THE
CONTEMPLATIVE
PRACTITIONER

THE CONTEMPLATIVE PRACTITIONER

Meditation in Education and the Professions

John P. Miller

OISE Press

The Ontario Institute for Studies in Education

The Ontario Institute for Studies in Education has three prime functions: to conduct programs of graduate study in education, to undertake research in education, and to assist in the implementation of the findings of educational studies. The Institute is a college chartered by an Act of the Ontario Legislature in 1965. It is affiliated with the University of Toronto for graduate studies purposes.

The publications program of the Institute has been established to make available information and materials arising from studies in education, to foster the spirit of critical inquiry, and to provide a forum for the exchange of ideas about education. The opinions expressed should be viewed as those of the contributors.

©The Ontario Institute for Studies in Education 1994
252 Bloor Street West
Toronto, Ontario
M5S   1V6

Canadian Cataloguing in Publication Data

Miller, John P.
    The contemplative practitioner : meditation in education and the professions

Includes bibliographical references and index.
ISBN 0–7744–0414–0

1. Meditation.   2. Education, Higher - North America.
3. Educators - Religious life.   4. College students -
Religious life.   I. Title.

BL627.M55 1994   291-4'3   C94–931540–0

ISBN: 0–7744–0414–0

1 2 3 4 5 MV 89 79 69 59 49

Copyright Acknowledgments

Chapter 2 was taken from an article coauthored by John P. Miller with his wife, Susan Drake, entitled "Beyond Reflection to Being: The Comtemplative Practitioner" in *Phenomenology and Pedagogy*, 9(1991):319–334.

Chapter 4 was adapted from an article by John P. Milier entitled "Contemplative Practice in Higher Education: An Experiment in Teacher Development" in the *Journal of Humanistic Psychology*, in press, and is reprinted with permission of Sage Publishers.

Selected excerpts from pages 6, 25, 39, and 41 from *Tao Te Ching* by Stephen Mitchell. Copyright © 1988 Stephen Mitchell. Reprinted by permission of HarperCollins Publishers, Inc.

Illustrations in Chapter 4 by Ken Herman.

Contents

Preface   vii

1.   Contemplation and Modern Life   1

2.   Reflection and Contemplation   17

3.   The Invisible World   33

4.   Contemplative Practice: Meditation   51

5.   Contemplatives and Their Practices   87

6.   Contemplative Practice in Higher Education   119

7.   The Contemplative Practitioner   135

Index   163

Preface

Donald Schon's concept of reflective practice has become an important part of current dialogue regarding professional development. His work has encouraged people to move away from mechanistic approaches to their work to the use of intuition and reflection in improving their practices. As valuable as this work is, I believe there is something missing in Schon's approach. Simply put, reflection is still rooted in a dualistic view of reality in that there is a subject that reflects on an object. If we stay with a dualistic view of reality, we ultimately end up with a fragmented and compartmentalized approach to life. Yes, there is a need for analysis and reflection, but there is also a need for synthesis and contemplation. Contemplation is characterized by a merging of subject and object. As I contemplate a sunset or a flower, separateness disappears and for a moment I can become the object I contemplate. Duality disappears. Contemplation is based on the notion of a deeply interconnected reality as described in subatomic physics and ecology. It is through contemplation that we can see, or envision, the Whole. In reflection we are still limited to focusing on the part. Of course, we need to be able to see the part and the whole, but our world, particularly the Western world, has focused mostly on the part. Through contemplation there is the opportunity to restore a balance between part and whole.

Through contemplation we are also able to tap a deeper energy that can bring joy and purpose to our work. By being more attentive to the smallest detail, which is the essence of contemplation, we experience time and space differently. We move into what Csikszentmihalyi calls the *flow experience* where we merge with what we are doing. Artists and athletes frequently report on the flow experience. However, I believe this heightened state should not be limited to certain artists and athletes, but is available to any professional through contemplation. The thesis of this book is that work and daily life can be enhanced immeasurably through contemplative practice. Emerson sums up the contemplative life very well, noting that the contemplative:

> will weave no longer a spotted life of shreds and patches, but he will live with a divine unity. He will cease from what is base and frivolous in his life, and be content with all places and any service he can render. He will calmly front the morrow in the negligency of that trust which carries God with it, and so hath already the whole future in the bottom of the heart. (Cited in Whelan, 1991, p. 25)

In the first three chapters I describe the nature of contemplation. More particularly, contemplation is compared to reflection in chapter 2, and its relation to spirituality is discussed in chapter 3. Meditation, which is a more structured form of contemplation, is described in chapter 4. In chapter 5 I briefly present the lives of five contemplatives—Buddha, Teresa of Avila, Emerson, Gandhi, and Merton—as it is important to see various forms of contemplation reflected in different individuals and traditions. In the next chapter I discuss my own experience in using meditation in the classes I teach in graduate courses in education. Finally, in the last chapter I describe how individuals in other professions such as medicine integrate contemplation into their work. I also outline a program for bringing contemplation into daily life.

A book has its own set of connections. First I must express my gratitude to all the teachers who have shown me the way in my own contemplative practice. Particularly important have been Ram Dass, Joseph Goldstein, Jack Kornfield, Christopher Titmuss, and U. Silananda. All of these individuals have helped and inspired my own practice immeasurably.

I also would like to thank many students who have taken my courses at the Ontario Institute for Studies in Education (OISE) and have worked with meditation. I have witnessed profound changes in the lives of many of these students, and this has also been an inspiration to me. I would also like to thank OISE for granting me the leave that enabled me to complete this book.

My appreciation also goes to those who helped with the typing and editing of this manuscript. Thanks to Barbara Drewette and Joan Graziani, who both typed this book. I would like to thank Lynn Flint at Bergin and Garvey and Hugh Oliver, Anne Nicholson, and John McConnell at OISE for their continued help and support.

THE
CONTEMPLATIVE
PRACTITIONER

1

Contemplation and Modern Life

Contemplation seems alien to modern life. Our life today tends to be hurried and task oriented. We often find that each day we have a long list of things to do with little time to do them. The demands just to keep up can be overwhelming.

In contrast, contemplation is not task oriented. Although there are long-term expectations, normally contemplation is not practiced to achieve something immediate. With so much to do, simply sitting still seems counter to the whole direction of modern life. Yet despite this apparent incongruity, many people who undertake some form of contemplative practice find that their lives become less fragmented. Many who have practiced meditation also comment that it makes them feel less isolated and more connected to the social and organic environment around them.

Thus, what seems so alien to modern life may be profoundly healing. As life speeds up, we feel the need to slow down. As we are constantly confronted with external stimuli, we find that we need to turn inward. As we are called on to be more linear and rational, we find that the intuitive response is sometimes more appropriate. As the noise increases, silence beckons. Most important, as we find society becoming more fragmented, we find that we need to be more connected.

WHAT IS CONTEMPLATION?

Contemplation involves the development of compassionate attention. Today our attention is pulled in a multitude of directions through technology and the media. We rarely seem to experience what Krishnamurti (1969) referred to when he said: "When you look totally you will give your whole attention, your whole being, everything of yourself, your eyes, your ears, your nerves. You will attend with complete self abandonment" (p. 31).

When we attend to the world in the manner suggested by Krishnamurti, we begin to see and relate to our environment in a different way. In fragmented consciousness we are pushed and pulled by the outside world; from contemplative awareness we see things as they are in the here and now. This type of awareness has also been called the flow experience (Csikszentmihalyi & Csikszentmihalyi, 1988). The flow experience is characterized by deep concentration where we lose, temporarily, the awareness of our separate self (e.g., the ego) and become totally focused on what we are doing. When we are fully attentive, we are also more likely to experience a sense of the sacred. For example, Csikszentmihalyi (1988), who has done research on the flow experience, notes:

> The climber feels at one with the mountain, the clouds, the rays of the sun, and the tiny bugs moving in and out of the shadow of the fingers holding to the rock; the surgeon feels at one with the movements of the operating team, sharing the beauty and the power of a harmonious transpersonal system. (p. 33)

When we experience the sacred moment, we don't need anything else. The experience is satisfying in and of itself; we become totally attuned to what is happening in the moment. Thomas Merton has described the sacred nature of contemplation.

> Contemplation is the highest expression of man's intellectual and spiritual life. It is that life itself, fully awake, fully active, fully aware that it is alive. It is spiritual wonder. It is spontaneous awe at the sacredness of life, of being. It is gratitude for life, for awareness and for being. It is a vivid realization of the fact that life and

being in us proceed from an invisible, transcendent and
infinitely abundant Source. (p. 1)

Contemplation in Merton's view involves a reconnecting with the
fundamental unity of life,or what Merton identifies as the Source. This
Source is the unity that underlies all life and is also known as God
(Christianity), Allah (Islam), the Tao (Taoism), the Brahman
(Hinduism), the realm of the invisible (Plato), the collective unconscious (Jung), and the implicate order (Bohm). This nonvisible world is
discussed more fully in chapter 4. The Christian contemplative David
Steindl-Rast (Bodian, 1985) has simply called this source "home." The
sense of being at home in the universe is found in children and in
adults who may "experience it sometimes in nature, or with other
human beings." Steindl-Rast states, "This longing for belonging, this
homing instinct of the heart, is the path within every path" (p. 27).
Contemplation, then, can be viewed as the way to be "at home."

Contemplation is characterized by a radical openness in which the
individual does not try to control what is happening. In Steindl-Rast's
words:

> Then comes a higher stage called "contemplation,"
> where you are no longer in control of the process.
> Instead, you open yourself, you drop the word or pas-
> sage or the image you've been dealing with, and you're
> just *there*. (Cited in Bodian, p. 28)

In this book, contemplation is conceived as nondualistic experience. For example, in reflection we reflect on an object, while in contemplation we tend to merge with the object. For a moment we become
the object or the process that we are contemplating.

Meditation is a form of contemplation that involves concentrated
practice. Meditation refers to many types of practice, such as vipassana,
or insight meditation, visualization, and mantra. Contemplation
includes meditation as well as spontaneous and unstructured moments
when we experience a connection with the unity of things. Patricia
Carrington (1977) has described some of these spontaneous moments.

> A mother holding her infant close is united with the
> child in a gentle rhythm as she rocks and sings to it.

A traveler leaning against a tree listens to the sounds of the breeze rustling the tree tops and barely senses his own breath; it is as though he had "become" the wind.

An elderly Jew, draped in his impressively trimmed prayer shawl and black cubes of leather *(tefillin)* sways back and forth in the dawn light, monotonously repeating a simple prayer which brings him exaltation.

A vacationer lies on the beach, giving herself over quietly to the sun and the air, engulfed by the lulling rhythms of the sea.

A man hears organ tones cascading through a cathedral; as they vibrate through him, he is carried into a reverie where memories and images of childhood flood him—he has become a child again.

A camper gazes into a lowering fire following the trail of the glowing ashes as they drift upward and fade into darkness; she feels as though she, too, were floating gently through space.

A rock climber on a mountaintop breathes in the silence above the earth; he is shaken by its immensity and his mind becomes as still as the snows in the mountain passes. (p. 3-4)

Contemplation, then, is the state of consciousness where we are deeply attentive and often experience a sense of awe and wonder.

RATIONALE FOR CONTEMPLATION

There is a substantial amount of research that indicates the positive benefits of meditation. Michael Murphy (1992) has summarized much of this research. For example, meditation helps in reducing the heart rate, lowering blood pressure, relaxing the muscles, heightening perception, improving motor skills, and improving empathy.

Jon Kabat-Zinn has helped large numbers of people deal with chronic pain at his clinic in Worcester, Massachusetts. The Kabat-Zinn work is particularly interesting because he has applied meditation within a mainstream setting. There is nothing New Age about his approach. His clinic is in a hospital, and almost all of his patients have been referred by doctors. Most of these patients had explored all traditional medical therapies and had come to Kabat-Zinn as a last resort. Kabat-Zinn has documented his work in his book *Full Catastrophe Living* (1990) and provided evidence of how the large majority of people found meditation helpful in dealing with the pain. In many cases the pain was relieved, and in other cases where the pain didn't go away, the patients found that they could deal with the pain much better.

Other interesting research has been conducted by Csikszentmihalyi (1988) on the flow experience. His work indicates that this state is an optimal state for performing any task. In other words, when we are deeply attentive, we are most likely to enjoy our work and do it well. The research on the flow experience shows one important link between contemplation and daily life. Deeply focused attention is the mode where we function most effectively in our work. In study and work we often find that we can feel very distracted, and as result our productivity suffers. We hear much today about competitiveness and productivity; often the attempt to improve productivity includes motivation through fear or rewards. A much more natural way to facilitate productivity is to cultivate the flow experience. Contemplation can help us experience the flow state more often and as a result participate more fully in our work. From the contemplative state our work becomes sacred in that it becomes fulfilling in itself. Traditionally, work has been treated as a means to an end; from a contemplative perspective it is an end in itself.

I believe the integration of spiritual practices such as meditation into daily life is part of the process of global awakening. At the heart of this awakening is a growing sense of the sacred quality of existence. Interestingly, some well-known scientists such as Carl Sagan and Stephen Jay Gould signed a statement titled "Preserving and Cherishing the Earth: An Appeal for Joint Commitment in Science and Religion." At one point the statement says:

> As scientists, many of us have had profound experiences of awe and reverence before the universe. We understand that what is regarded as sacred is more likely to be treated with care and respect. Our planetary home should be so regarded. Efforts to safeguard and cherish the environment need to be infused with a vision of the sacred. (Cited in Knudtson & Suzuki, 1992, p. 182)

To view the universe with "awe and reverence" is, in fact, to contemplate the universe. If mainstream scientists are proclaiming the importance of the sacred, we are witnessing a significant shift from scientific materialism to a more holistic perspective. This shift is most noticeable in the environmental movement. Mainstream politicians such as Al Gore (1992) are also referring to the link between the global crisis and inner transformation:

> The more deeply I search for the roots of the global
> environmental crisis, the more I am convinced that it is
> an outer manifestation of an inner crisis that is, for lack
> of a better word, spiritual. . . . I have come to believe in
> the value of a kind of inner ecology that relies on the
> same principles of balance and holism that characterize
> a healthy environment. (p. 12, 367)

Contemplation allows the individual to gradually overcome his or her sense of separateness. Our society reinforces the personal ego, which spends most of the day planning, striving, and competing. Our ego arises from the various social roles we engage in, such as parent, worker, and spouse. The extent to which we identify with these roles is also the extent of our suffering. For example, if people invest their whole identity in their work (e.g., the workaholic), they find it extremely difficult to adjust when they retire. The father who is too attached to his role as father may have a difficult time letting go of his son or daughter when he or she leaves home. Almost every spiritual tradition focuses on letting go of ego and letting our Self, Atman or Buddha-Nature naturally arise.

I like Emerson's (1909-1914) conception of the ego and the Self, which he wrote in his journal:

> A man finds out that there is somewhat in him that
> knows more than he does. Then he comes presently to
> the curious question, Who's who? which of these two is
> really me? the one that knows more or the one that
> knows less; the little fellow or the big fellow? (Vol. 9, p.
> 190)

The little fellow is our ego, which so desperately tries to manipulate the universe according to its own ends, while the big fellow is our true

Self, which is in accord with the harmony of things. Gabriel Marcel said that the deeper we go within ourselves, the more we find that which is beyond ourselves.

The social structure we live in continually reinforces the ego through competition and fear. Thus, we constantly are trying to gain an edge on others in our work, on the highway, or when we stand in line at the post office or the grocery store. Meditation lets us witness the striving of the ego. During meditation practice, we compassionately witness all our thoughts and ego trips, and very gradually we begin to see that our fundamental identity is not the thoughts that form our ego structure but that clear awareness that is witnessing the arising and falling of all these thoughts. This basic insight is the beginning of liberation and compassion.

Finally, I would say that contemplation allows us to experience true joy. Because it allows us to see our life and work in a new and fresh manner, we take delight in the little things. Blue sky, cloud formations, flowers, children at play provide endless sources of surprise and delight. Yes, the openness that comes through meditation also increases our sensitivity to pain and suffering, but at the same time this openness can allow our hearts to sing. Through contemplation we come to know that all pain is temporary and that underlying the transient nature of life is something so grand and vast that it makes us smile. I would like to quote one of my students who wrote about joy in her journal after a meditation session:

> I concentrated on my breathing patterns and I slipped into my familiar stance. Little entered my mind, I was simply enjoying the sensations of peace and tranquility. When I awoke, I left the apartment and walked home. I noticed that I was humming and strolling with a light step. Children on their bicycles and little puppies in my path were making me smile. In this remote corner of the world, all was calm. I realized after a while that I was mirroring the image of my surroundings and in a small way, it felt wonderful to be a part of the serenity of life. . . .
>
> In essence, I felt that I have participated in an education of introspection, as well as the experience of interconnectedness with other people, with the surrounding nature, and with the infinite universe.

We can get this same feeling of connection from simply listening to a Mozart piano concerto, a Haydn symphony, a Beethoven string quartet or a Schubert song. Each of these composers knew the deepest pain, but their music calls forth from us joy, delight, and the sense that underlying all the pain and suffering there is an unseen harmony.

A PERSONAL VIEW

I have been practicing meditation since 1974. In recent years, however, I noticed that the barrier between my private inner work and my public activities has been dissolving. I work and teach at the Ontario Institute for Studies in Education mostly in the area of holistic education. I teach courses in holistic education and contemplation, and since 1988 I have asked my students to meditate as part of the courses I teach. This work is discussed in chapter 6. I introduced meditation into my class because I believe that teaching based in the Self is much more rewarding and fulfilling than ego-based teaching. Students keep journals to report on their practice, and approximately 400 students, mostly experienced teachers and administrators, reported the powerful impact of meditation on their own lives. Many students have indicated to me that they have continued their practice after the course is over. Almost all the students begin to see the connection between pursuing some form of inner practice and performing their work. This book is largely motivated by the experience with them as several of my students have found that meditation is a transforming experience. One woman commented:

> This course has been a holistic experience for me. It has changed me fundamentally in the way I live my life. I am meditating for the first time in my life, and I see a calmness and a stability that emerges from that time.

One man commented:

> I am still amazed at how I now handle situations which formerly were sources of irritation and anxiety. I attribute this to the peacefulness, relaxation, and seren-ity associatd with meditation. Meditating daily has

changed me. I am a happier, more clearly focused per-
son.

For most of my students, meditation is a new experience, and they are skeptical about the process. The man above commented:

I laugh now when I think back to the thoughts I had
when you first mentioned that we were required to medi-
tate daily and keep a journal of the same. Though I
didn't truly believe that it would be of any assistance, I
decided that I was going to give it my best shot.
Initially, I was shocked with what was happening. I
wouldn't believe myself. . . . I will continue to meditate
regularly since I have found nothing else I have per-
formed on a regular basis to be as powerful.

Most of my students feel that meditation has helped them in their work, as they can now cope with the stress of teaching. The connection between contemplation and other professions such as medicine is also occurring; I have already referred to the work of Jon Kabat-Zinn. Peter Senge, in his book *The Fifth Discipline* (1990), suggests that workers in organizations need to develop personal mastery through meditation. Combined with other organizational changes, personal mastery can let individuals and businesses become learning organizations that have a much better chance to survive and even flourish in today's fragile economy.

I believe that the interest in contemplation is related to other changes that are happening on this planet. It is possible to look at these changes in terms of polarities. The changes in organizations, medicine and education are an attempt to achieve proper alignment of these polarities. The following list on the left represents qualities that have been predominant in the Western industrialized world. The list on the right, I believe, represents emergent qualities that are ascending and coming into balance, or appropriate relationship, with the qualities on the left.

Masculine	Feminine
Independent	Interdependent
Quantity	Quality
Outer	Inner
Rational	Intuitive

Economy	Environment
Hierarchy	Network
Technology	Consciousness
Material	Sacred
Nation	Globe or Region

In examining these polarities it is important to understand that the qualities on the right are coming into appropriate relationship with those on the right. One should not view one set of qualities as "bad" or the other as "good." Problems and suffering arise when one set of qualities overwhelms the other, leading to dominance and repression. A much healthier scenario is when we have *balance* or appropriate relationship between these qualities.

Masculine/Feminine

Some scholars (Tarnas, 1991) have identified feminism as the most important movement of this century. This has involved not only the emergence of women into leadership positions in society but also the start of women's assumption of roles normally held by men. At the same time, qualities associated with females such as intuition and caring are also viewed as being important for all human beings.

Not only has feminism been part of this polarity, but the whole realm of sexuality is being reexamined. Not only are we looking at what it means to be female, but writers such as Bly and others are exploring what it means to be male. Sexual roles are being redefined and expanded. It should be noted here that as the qualities in the right-hand column ascend, their ascendency is viewed fearfully by people identified with forces on the left. This fear has led to violence against women. As the qualities listed come into appropriate relationship, there is often violence or conflict.

Independent/Interdependent

Western industrialized society has cultivated independence and autonomy as values. This can be seen in the extreme by the ideal of the "rugged individual" in the United States (e.g., John Wayne) as well as in the moral scales developed by Kohlberg and Piaget, in which autonomy is at the top. Now there is more concern about how mutuality can arise within a group setting, and there is a perception that the individual is not an island but is connected to something much larger. Systems thinking and quality circles reflect this trend in business while the move toward cooperative learning demonstrates this development in education.

Quantity/Quality

Western industrialized society has stressed quantity with an emphasis on GNP, profit margins, and standardized tests in schools. However, in the last fifteen years there has been a movement toward qualitative assessment, which focuses on meaning and interpretation rather than number crunching.

Outer/Inner

Behavioral psychology dominated psychology for much of this century. Although behavioral psychology has now given way to cognitive psychology, there has been a strong emphasis on the observable. In business and technology, inputs and outputs are stressed, while product is viewed as much more important than process.

In contrast, there is the view that the outer world is a reflection of our inner world. In other words, if our consciousness is filled with greed and aversion, then the world will simply manifest these qualities. Various forms of contemplation acknowledge this and allow us to work on our inner life. As we "clean up" our inner life, there is a greater chance the environment will also become cleaner.

Rational/Intuitive

Until very recently, we have supported the rational, linear approach, particularly when it was endorsed by the expert. We have tended to deny our own hunches or deeper intuitions. The rational problem-solver was seen as the ideal as the "best and brightest" were brought together to solve problems like Vietnam and poverty. However, we have learned from the sixties that flow charts and mathematical models often do not take into account the unseen, the unusual, or the idiosyncratic. John Eisenberg in his book, *The Limits of Reason* (1992), has brilliantly shown how "rational" approaches to education, law, and morality are, at best, naive and, at worst, dangerous. By accessing our intuitions, we sometimes can come to a deeper level of understanding where we can gain a more holistic way of dealing with problems.

Economy/Environment

Western industrialized society has continued to stress economic growth. However, we are beginning to witness the limits of that growth as the ozone hole becomes larger, acid rain increases, and global warming continues. Until the last couple of decades, we did not consider the environmental consequences of our economic activity. Now we are being forced to examine the relationship between our economic activity and the environment. The environmental crisis has made us look at how everything we do is connected and has an impact on the world around us. In short, as the hole in the ozone layer increases and global warming becomes worse we are being forced to adopt an ecological or holistic perspective if we want to insure our survival.

Hierarchy/Network

The model for organizations in Western industrialized society has been the ladder. People have to work their way up if they want to succeed. In psychology our models of development, particularly Piaget's and Kohlberg's, are also hierarchical. Organizationally there has been a move toward the flat-line organization. Tom Peters (1992) and others talk about organizations with small decentralized units that function closely as a group within the larger organization. Organizations, however, cannot become too decentralized. They need common purpose as well as a conception of how each unit is part of a whole. Again, we are searching for the right relationship between the vertical and the horizontal in systems and organizations.

Technology/Consciousness

Western industrialized culture has become a culture of technique. We are fascinated by gadgets and technologies, and in many cases these technologies have enhanced our life. Computers and various forms of media are helping make the global village a reality. At the same time, these technologies shape our interactions in ways that we are not fully aware of.

Thomas Berry (1988) has warned that we are caught in a technological trance where we always look for the technological solution. In contrast, it may be more appropriate to look at the consciousness that we bring to the technology. If our consciousness tends to be fragmented and filled with greed and aversion, then technology will simply reinforce the fragmentation. If we are fully aware as we use the technology, there is much greater chance that its use will be appropriate.

Material/Sacred

Materialism has dominated the twentieth century as Western industrialized society continues to seek every form of material comfort. As the comforts have increased, we have become skeptical of anything we cannot see or touch. Related to materialism has been the rise of instrumentalism, or the use of something or somebody to acquire something else.

In contrast, the notion of the sacred involves a sense that all life and the earth itself has an inherent sacred quality and should not be used in an instrumental manner but instead should be viewed with reverence. This polarity does not deny the importance of material comfort, but again the prevailing way of life in Western industrialized culture has diminished a sense of the sacred. However, today the environmental movement and interest in indigenous people's spirituality has awakened a renewed sense of reverence for life and the nonmaterial.

Nation/Globe or Region

The nation-state, which has been the predominant geopolitical force since the Middle Ages, is being pulled apart. At one level there is more allegiance to regions based on cultural and linguistic factors. These changes are most obvious in central Europe and the former Soviet Union, but any country that has some sort of linguistic or cultural minority can feel the pull. Another force is globalism. Free trade is forcing the economies to become more global, while organizations such as the United Nations seem to be gaining prominence in the post-cold-war world. We don't know what new world order will emerge but global agencies should continue to play a major role in adjudicating disputes and dealing with various social and health issues.

Despite the problems that exist, such as drugs, unemployment, violence, and abuse, each day I am struck by the positive changes taking place on the planet. These changes include those just noted above as well as the decline of the nuclear threat, the explosion of democratic governments around the world, and the interest in indigenous peoples' approach to life. In many ways we are beginning to come to our senses. As a human race we are beginning to connect with each other, to the planet, and to something larger than ourselves. The more deeply we open ourselves to these connections, the more likely fundamental healing change can begin to take place on the planet. Contemplation is integral to this process of healing and awakening.

REFERENCES

Berry, T. (1988). *The Dream of the Earth.* San Francisco: Sierra Books.

Bodian, S. (1985, May/June). The heart of prayer: An interview with Christian contemplative David Steindl-Rast. *Yoga Journal,* pp. 25-28.

Carrington, p. (1977). *Freedom in meditation.* Garden City, NY: Anchor Press.

Csikszentmihalyi, M. (1988). The flow experience and human psychology. In M. Csikszentmihalyi and I. S. Csikszentmihalyi (Eds.), *Optimal experience: Psychological studies of flow in consciousness.* Cambridge: Cambridge University Press.

Csikszentmihalyi, M., & Csikszentmihalyi, I. S. (Eds.) (1988). *Optimal experience: Psychological studies of flow in consciousness.* Cambridge: Cambridge University Press.

Eisenberg, J. (1992). *The limits of reason: Indeterminacy in law, education, and morality.* Toronto: OISE Press.

Emerson, R. W. (1909-14). *The journals of Ralph Waldo Emerson.* Edward Waldo Emerson & Waldo Emerson Forbes (Eds.) Vol. 9, Boston and New York: Houghton Mifflin.

Gore, A. (1992). *Earth in the balance: Ecology and the human spirit.* Boston: Houghton Mifflin.

Kabat-Zinn, J. (1990). *Full catastrophe living: Using the wisdom of your body and mind to face stress, pain and illness.* New York: Delacorte Press.

Krishnamurti, J. (1969). *Freedom from the known.* New York: Harper & Row.

Knudtson, p., & Suzuki, D. (1992). *Wisdom of the elders.* Toronto: Stoddart.

Merton, T. (1972). *New seeds of contemplation.* New York: New Directions.

Murphy, M. (1992). *The future of the body: Explorations into the further evolution of human nature.* New York: Jeremy Tarcher.

Peters, T. p. (1992). *Liberation management necessary management: Necessary disorganization for the nanosecond nineties.* New York: Alfred A. Knopf.

Senge, p. M. (1990). *The fifth discipline: The art and practice of the learning organization.* New York: Doubleday.

Tarnas, R. (1991). *The passion of the Western mind: Understanding the ideas that have shaped our world view.* New York: Harmony.

Whelan, R. (Ed.) (1991). *Self-reliance: The wisdom of Ralph Waldo Emerson as inspiration for daily living.* New York: Bell Tower.

2

Reflection and Contemplation

Schon's book *The Reflective Practitioner* (1983) has facilitated much needed discourse about how individuals working in different professions can reflect on their own practice. Schon argues that the best professional practice is based on reflection. This concept of the reflective practitioner has encouraged people in the professions to view their work as more than mastery of content and technical competence. Although Schon's work is extremely valuable, I believe that there is yet another level beyond the reflective practitioner where the person can "live" his or her practice; this is the level of the contemplative practitioner.

Schon claims that the professions have tended toward Technical Rationality. At this level, education, for example, is simply the recall of knowledge and mastery of technique. According to Schon, Technical Rationality is rooted in positivism, which rests on the premise that empirical science provides the best model for all inquiry and practice. Thus empiricism has been used as the model not only for the sciences, but for the social sciences and even areas such as philosophy. One of the principal thrusts of twentieth-century philosophy has been an analytic philosophy that rests on positivistic assumptions and abandons metaphysics as nonsensical.

Technical Rationality involves instrumental problem solving and "depends on agreement about ends" (Schon, 1983, p. 41). To solve problems, the person immersed in Technical Rationality usually relies on a model that often is not directly related to practice. Schein (1973) argues that there are three components for professional knowledge based on a positivistic framework that is hierarchic in nature. The basic science component is deemed to be the most important.

1. An *underlying discipline* or *basic science* component upon which practice rests or from which it is developed.
2. An *applied science* or *"engineering"* component from which many of the day-to-day diagnostic procedures and problem-solving solutions are derived.
3. A *skills and attitudinal* component that concerns the actual performance of services to the client, using the underlying basic and applied knowledge. (p. 43)

From the Technical Rationality perspective, the professions are viewed as applied sciences, which are deemed to have less status than the pure sciences. For example, Greenwood (1966) argues that the scientific method is needed to bolster social work as a profession.

> To generate valid theory that will provide a solid base for professional techniques requires the application of the scientific method to the service related problems of the profession. Continued employment of the scientific method is nurtured by and in turn reinforces the element of rationality. (p. 11)

From the Technical Rationality perspective, the professions are based on science, from which the professional learns the more practical skills. These skills are viewed as having lesser status than the knowledge based on the scientific method.

Schon (1983) argues that Technical Rationality has not worked because abstract theory does not inform practice. Practitioners are confronted with problematic situations that are characterized by uncertainty, disorder, and indeterminacy. They can become uncomfortable when they can't account for what they do according to theory. The effective practitioner, instead, operates more intuitively and makes changes based on moment-to-moment decisions. As Bernstein (1976) has written, the view of science from a Technical Rationality perspective is inadequate even at the theoretical level.

> There is not a single major thesis advanced by either nineteenth-century Positivists or the Vienna Circle that

has not been devastatingly criticized when measured by the Positivists' own standards for philosophical argument. The original formulations of the analytic-synthetic dichotomy and the verifiability criterion of meaning have been abandoned. It has been effectively shown that Positivists' understanding of the natural sciences and the formal disciplines is grossly oversimplified. (p. 207)

Following Schon's argument, the technical approach to teaching has not been effective either. Teachers constantly find themselves in new situations without precedent. Erdman (1987) suggests that teaching, by its very nature, pushes educators into areas of ambiguity and uncertainty. From this perspective, the technical approach to teaching is simply inadequate because it is not flexible enough.

REFLECTION-IN-ACTION

As an alternative to Technical Rationality, Schon (1983) presents his view of reflection as a more artistic, intuitive process. Embedded in his conception of reflection is Polanyi's (1962) tacit knowing, which involves an intuitive sense of how to do things that cannot always be explained in explicitly conceptual terms. Polyani states "the aim of a skillful performance is achieved by the observance of a set of rules which are not known as such to the person following them" (p. 49). Reflection-in-action, then, refers to a skillful performance that tends to have the following qualities:

- There are actions, recognitions, and judgments which we know how to carry out spontaneously; we do not have to think about them prior to or during their performance.
- We are often unaware of having learned to do these things; we simply find ourselves doing them.
- In some cases, we were once aware of the understandings which were subsequently internalized in our feeling for the stuff of action. In other cases, we may never have been aware of them. In both cases, however, we are usually unable to describe the knowing which our action reveals. (p. 54)

Schon (1983) cites examples from baseball and music to explain his point. For example, the pitcher in baseball is constantly making adjustments to keep ahead of the hitters. He will change speeds and move the ball to different locations, and this process tends to be intuitive rather than rational. In jazz, the players will improvise in a spontaneous way as they collectively develop a feel for the music and what combination of notes is appropriate at different moments. In teaching, the teacher will shift gears in the lesson plan, based on an intuition of what is right, to reach the student in a particular situation if he or she comes to a "teachable moment."

Reflection-in-action can focus on a variety of elements. The practitioner, for example, may deal with the tacit norms underlying a particular decision or on the appropriate strategy that is implicit in his or her behavior. Alternatively, the practitioner may reflect on the right feeling that can develop in approaching a problem, on the way he or she has framed a problem, or on the appropriate role to play in solving the problem. In short, reflection in action weaves together practice and theory at an intuitive level.

The reflective practitioner may reframe the problem several times, as the setting of the problem is probably more important than the problem-solving procedures themselves. For example, Schon (1983) states that 80 to 85 percent of cases faced by an ophthalmologist do not fall into the "book" of standard diagnosis. The doctor must constantly look for new ways to diagnose and treat cases that arise. Likewise, the teacher is always being confronted with new situations that require new solutions.

Schon (1983) quotes Tolstoy to give an example of reflection-in-action in education:

> Every individual must, in order to acquire the art of reading in the shortest possible time, be taught quite apart from any other, and therefore there must be a separate method for each. That which forms an insuperable difficulty to one does not in the least keep back another, and vice versa. One pupil has a good memory, and it is easier for him to memorize the syllables than to comprehend the vowellessness of the consonants; another reflects calmly and will comprehend a most rational sound method; another has a fine instinct, and he grasps

the law of word combinations by reading whole words at a time.

The best teacher will be he who has at his tongue's end the explanation of what it is that is bothering the pupil. These explanations give the teacher the knowledge of the greatest possible number of methods, the ability of inventing new methods and, above all, not a blind adherence to one method but the conviction that all methods are one-sided, and that the best method would be the one which would answer best to all the possible difficulties incurred by a pupil, that is, not a method but an art and talent.

Every teacher must . . . . by regarding every imperfection in the pupil's comprehension, not as a defect of the pupil, but as a defect of his own instruction, endeavor to develop in himself the ability of discovering new methods. (pp. 65-66)

In a sense the teacher is an on-the-spot researcher who must be ready with new methods based on an intuitive sense of what is appropriate for the student that he or she is dealing with. As a result of this notion, researchers at the Massachusetts Institute of Technology have undertaken a program of in-service education for teachers based on the idea of reflection-in-action (Schon, 1983, p. 66). Educators (Holmes Group, 1990; Fullan & Connelly, 1987) are advocating teacher reform based on the concept of the reflective practitioner.

BEING AND CONTEMPLATION

But is reflection enough? I would argue that there is an element that is necessary to good practice that is not included in the notion of reflection. This is the quality of Being or Presence. Perhaps the best example of Presence comes from music, as it is not enough for a pianist just to be a good technician or even to play the music with the right intuitive sense. In listening to music we look for more than technique and musicianship; we also seek to be moved, and it is the musician's depth of character or Being that raises the performance to that level. Certainly what draws us to a Horowitz or Ashkenazy performance is not just the technical proficiency, but the depth and warmth of the performance.

Good teachers also evoke this quality of depth, a quality that Emerson (1965) so aptly captures in a talk he made to teachers:

> According to the depth from which you draw your life, such is the depth not only of your strenuous effort, but of your manners and presence. The beautiful nature of the world has here blended your happiness with your power. . . . Consent yourself to be an organ of your highest thought, and lo! suddenly you put all men in your debt, and are the fountain of an energy that goes pulsing on with waves of benefit to the borders of society, to the circumference of things. (p. 437)

Clearly we are talking about another level of experience that is beyond sense experience and even reflection. This third level adds to the holistic view of experience by connecting to Being. At this level, then, we also connect with a larger reality (e.g., the Tao, the Over-Soul, the Ground of Being) that is much different than the empiricist's notion of an objective reality or the conception of personal knowledge based on individual construction of meaning requiring commitment and reflection. This level, the level of the *contemplative practitioner*, is realized through various forms of contemplation such as meditation and myth.

Drawing on the thought of St. Bonaventure, a favorite philosopher of Western mystics, Wilber (1983) cites three levels of experience, which correspond to the levels discussed in this chapter: Technical Rationality, Reflection, and Being. Bonaventure describes three modes of knowing or three "eyes." The first eye is of the flesh, where we perceive the external world of space, time, and objects. The second eye is reason, where we know through philosophy, logic, and reflection. The third eye is that of contemplation, where we gain knowledge of transcendent realities. At this level the distinction between subject and object disappears. Wilber notes:

> Further, said St. Bonaventure, all knowledge is a type of *illumination*. There is exterior and inferior illumination (*lumen exterius* and *lumen inferius*), which lights the eye of flesh and gives us knowledge of sense objects. There

is *lumen interius*, which lights the eye of reason and gives us knowledge of philosophical truths. And there is *lumen superius*, the light of transcendent Being which illumines the eye of contemplation and reveals salutary truth, "truth which is unto liberation." (p. 3)

Wilber (1983) also states that Bonaventure's three levels correspond with the ideas of Hugh of St. Victor (first of the great Victorine mystics) who distinguished between *cogitatio, meditatio,* and *contemplatio. Cogitatio* is empiricism and thus is based on knowing the facts of the external world. *Meditatio* involves internal reflection and seeking the truths of the mind. *Contemplatio,* again, is beyond duality "whereby the psyche or soul is united instantly with Godhead in transcendent insight (revealed by the eye of contemplation)" (p. 3).

Although Wilber (1983) has cited Christian mystics, these three eyes can be found in other mystical and philosophical traditions. For example, the Hindus also speak of a third eye that, again, is the eye of Being. Kant spoke of three levels of knowing that correspond roughly to the levels cited above. Kant's three levels include: (1) sensibility, or sense experience; (2) understanding, or conceptual and scientific intelligence; and (3) reason, which intuits transcendent ideas.

Wilber (1983) claims that the three levels are nested and each of the three levels cited by Bonaventure and Hugh of St. Victor transcends the previous level. Thus the eye of the mind includes and transcends the eye of the flesh. The eye of mind includes sense experience but also contains ideas, images, concepts, and logic. At this level, we can reflect on our sense experience and use images and concepts to facilitate reflection. Also, we can confine ourselves to the level of the mind in an area such as mathematics. However, it is an error to reduce the level of reason to the level of flesh; this kind of reductionism ignores the unique features of each level. Thus contemplation transcends, yet includes, the previous two levels.

Consider the relationship between practice and theory. From the Technical Rationality viewpoint, theory is seen as separate from and superior to practice. Yet people working in the professions are often confused by a problematic situation where what they do does not fit the theory. Reflection-in-action answers this dilemma. Practice and theory are interwoven in a dialectical process of framing the problem and on-the-spot experimenting in a reflective conversation with the unique situation at hand. From the perspective of Being, there is a synthesis of theory and practice, and duality disappears. Theory and practice are experienced as a unity.

Being has been called the Self (Jung), the Atman (Hinduism), our Buddha-Nature (Buddhism), and the soul (Christianity). Merton (1959), the American Trappist monk, spoke of the "inner self," which is another description of Being:

> Instead of seeing the external world in its bewildering complexity, separateness, and multiplicity; instead of seeing objects as things to be manipulated for pleasure or profit; instead of placing ourselves over against objects in a posture of desire, defiance, suspicion, greed or fear, the inner self sees the world from a deeper and more spiritual viewpoint. In the language of Zen, it (the inner self) sees things "without affirmation or denial"; that is to say, from a higher vantage point, which is intuitive and concrete and which has no need to manipulate or distort reality by means of slanted concepts and judgments. It simply "sees" what it sees and does not take refuge behind a screen of conceptual prejudices and verbalistic distortions. (p. 17)

Merton (1959) speaks of intuition as an aspect of Being, but is this the same intuition as Schon's? Vaughan (1979) has spoken of levels of intuition, and three levels can be linked with Wilber's (1983) different eyes. The first level of intuition is what Vaughan calls a physical level, where the body or the flesh reacts instinctively to a situation. For example, muscle tension can indicate stress in person's life.

The next level is the mental, which parallels the eye of reason. At the mental level intuition is often expressed through images, just as we may have flashes of insight that can lead to inquiry. This level is similar to Schon's (1983) reflective practitioner level, where the individual uses moment-to-moment insight to help in the problem-solving process.

The highest level of intuition in Vaughan's (1979) framework is the spiritual, which parallels the eye of contemplation. Here intuition is independent from feelings, thoughts, and sensations. Vaughan comments: "Paradoxically, the cues on which intuition depend on the other levels are regarded as interference at this level" (p. 77). At this level, intuition moves beyond dualism to experience unity directly. The following statement by Teilhard de Chardin (1965) is an example of spiritual intuition.

> The farther and more deeply we penetrate into matter,
> by means of increasingly powerful methods, the more
> we are confounded by the interdependence of its parts.
> Each element of the cosmos is positively woven from all
> the others. . . . *It is impossible to cut into this network, to*
> *isolate a portion without it becoming frayed and*
> *unravelled at all its edges.* All around us, as far as the
> eye can see, the universe holds together, and only one
> way of considering it is really possible, that is, to take it
> as a whole, in one piece. (pp. 43-44)

Phenomenologically, Being is experienced as unmediated awareness. This awareness is characterized by openness, a sense of relatedness, and by awe and wonder. The sense of relatedness goes beyond Buber's I-Thou experience, where there is still a bipolar situation. When we experience Being, duality drops away and as teachers we see part of ourselves in our students. At the deepest level we may experience brief moments of communion with our students. For example, Freedman (1990) describes how one teacher, Jessica Siegel, has each of her high school students write an autobiography, and through this process she develops a communal bond with each student.

> Every year she finishes the autobiographies feeling the
> same way. Her students are heroes. . . . How they fill her
> with awe. How they, yes, inspire her. . . . When she reads
> their words, when she hears their voices, when she can
> practically grasp their urgent breath in this empty room,
> she knows her life has a reason. (pp. 68-69)

Teachers frequently speak of how their students can instill in them a sense of wonder. For example, Marcia Umland (Macrorie, 1984), an elementary school teacher states, "I get exhausted, but not burned out. Sometimes I'm dropping my dream for a day or two, but most days I'm on, and stunned by the kids" (p. 161). At this level we can see our students as Zen masters who with their directness can awaken us if we remain open. We need to keep the kind of openness suggested by Emerson (1965):

If a child happens to show that he knows any fact about astronomy, or planets, or birds, or rocks, or history that interests him and you, hush all the classes and encourage him to tell it so that all may hear. Then you have made your school-room like the world. Of course you will insist on modesty in the children and respect to their teachers, but if the boy stops you in your speech, cries out that you are wrong and sets you right, hug him! (pp. 226-227)

THE CONTEMPLATIVE PRACTITIONER

When we experience Being we tend to perceive quality in a more direct and open manner. Contemplation allows us to access Being and perceive reality in a new way. Buchman (1989) claims that contemplation includes "careful attention and quiet wonder" (p. 39). Buchman (1989) also cites Thomas Aquinas who believed that contemplation is more important than the active life in that the "return to the active life from the contemplative. is by way of direction, in that the active life is guided by the contemplative" (cited in Buchman, 1989, p. 39).

This book outlines various ways that we can become contemplative practitioners. One vehicle is meditation, which is described more fully in chapter 4. Another approach, which I will mention briefly in this chapter, is mythology.

MEDITATION

One time-honored contemplative practice is meditation. Meditation has been practiced for centuries in different psychological and spiritual traditions. Kornfield (Miller, J., 1988), who teaches Buddhist insight meditation, states:

Most of us are disconnected; we are disconnected from our hearts and our bodies, from the mind and its ways, from one another, from the earth and from the universal laws and truths. Through meditation we can reconnect with all of these factors. Through meditation we can rediscover love, oneness and freedom. Many people

> meditate for other reasons–for example, to deal with pain and to understand suffering. However, if one practices with an open heart and mind, meditation eventually leads to a oneness, a deep connectedness. (p. 130)

Meditation practice generally involves a quieting of the mind by focusing our attention on the in-out flow of the breath, counting our breaths, or reciting a simple phrase (mantra). The task of meditation tends to be rather simple, so we become attentive of what is happening both within and without. By quieting down, we begin gradually to watch and gradually to let go of the ego-chatter in our heads. It is the ego-chatter that forms the main barrier to our hearts, our Being. Ego-chatter can focus on such issues as how we can acquire material possessions, achieve a promotion, or control an interpersonal relationship. Traditionally, meditation practice usually allows us to see how the ego-chatter, or our thoughts, can control us. For example, during meditation the thought can arise that I need to buy that new jacket, and instead of simply reacting to the thought, I can simply watch it arise and disappear in my consciousness. Through meditation we learn that we can witness our thoughts rather than simply run on "automatic pilot," reacting unconsciously to our thoughts.

Is not meditation a form of reflection? The goal of meditation is to rest in that place that Merton (1959) referred to as beyond thought and concept–a place of direct awareness. In the meditation process, the focus is not on analyzing or reflecting on the thoughts, but on moving to a place of spacious awareness. In this place of direct awareness, the world can break through our ego barriers so that we feel a deep connectedness to the environment that surrounds us.

If we are lost in our ego-chatter, it is difficult for us to experience the world directly. Our thoughts and our ego form a barrier to the world and to our experience; through meditation we gradually dismantle the ego so that we see how things are. The ego is the source of our sense of separateness, and thus by gradually letting go of ego, we connect to others and the universe in a more direct and compassionate way. Deshimaru (1985), a Zen master, says: "Once the ego has disappeared there is no more duality. As soon as there is myself and others, that is duality. When there is no more me there are no more others; there is interdependence" (p. 19).

At an ego level, we tend to relate to others on the basis of our own needs. When things do not turn out the way we expect, we can become jealous, frustrated, and resentful. We can become involved in an emotional struggle to maintain ourselves in a particular way. Tremendous energy is exerted to maintain our view of how things should be rather than relating openly to the situation as it arises. In contrast, meditation can be used simply to relax the body and mind before a difficult work assignment.

The late Trungpa (1984), a Tibetan meditation master, describes how meditation leads to an open heart and compassion:

> When you slouch [in meditation], you are trying to hide your heart, trying to protect it by slumping over. But when you sit upright but relaxed in the posture of meditation, your heart is naked. Your entire being is exposed–to yourself, first of all, but to others as well. So through the practice of sitting still and following your breath as it goes out and dissolves, you are connecting with your heart. (p. 45)

Through meditation we can develop sensitivity, a basic compassion, or what Trungpa calls the "awakened heart."

Meditation, however, should not be restricted to sitting practice; rather it can infuse one's existence with a basic sense of connectedness. The person who meditates, then, can bring the same attention and groundedness that develops in sitting practice to his or her workplace. This centeredness and attentiveness can be part of living presence that others respond to.

NARRATIVE, PERSONAL MYTHOLOGY, UNIVERSAL MYTHOLOGY

Universal myths provide another context for contemplation. They allow us to connect our personal stories to the Big Story that is described in various mythologies. The Big Story is essentially the story of how we overcome the prison of the ego to realize the fullness of our Being.

The path of transformation should be a "path with heart." In Campbell's (1988) words, the path with heart is "following one's bliss." We can turn to mythology to discover an age-old map to guide us on the inner journey. Life stories can be embedded in a larger, more universal story. This larger framework grants a wider perspective from which to interpret the story and allows an understanding of the path to Being.

Over the ages myths from different cultures have continued to have the same symbolism and structure. This universality in patterns suggests that myths tap into the very essence of being human. They appeal to humans by connecting with our Being or that still, small voice of the heart. A story that has been replayed again and again across many cultures is the journey of the hero. Campbell (1949) has labeled the journey the "monomyth" and outlined a skeleton plot that illustrates how the story unfolds in much the same way in many myths. It is the story of an individual called to adventure who undergoes a series of tests or trials as a part of that adventure. Eventually, the individual receives a reward, and he or she must return to the world with the fruits of the reward. The final step is to share newfound knowledge, or serve others. The journey was taken by Jesus, Buddha, Moses, Dante, and many of the mythological heroes and heroines from most cultures. "But essentially, everyone's story is the same. It's the story of the hero's or heroine's journey" (Miller, R., 1988, p. 43).

The journey can be viewed metaphorically as a map of personal transformation (Campbell, 1988). The call to adventure means one must leave behind the world as one knows it. This step into the unknown is followed by a series of obstacles or trials that are usually self-created by ego attachments. As someone undergoes the tests, there is illumination or learning from the suffering and pain. Ultimately, there is the reward: a personal transformation or change in identity as the individual has reached a new level of consciousness. Finally, one must return to the world with this new awareness.

Campbell (1949) suggests that it possible to look at the lives of the great teachers metaphorically; that is, we can relate their journeys to our own experiences. For example, consider the time the Buddha sat meditating under the Bodhi tree and was tempted to break his concentration by Kama-Mara, the god of love and death.

> The dangerous god appeared mounted on an elephant and carrying weapons in his thousand hands. He was surrounded by his army, which extended twelve leagues before him, twelve to the right, twelve to the left, and in the rear as far as to the confines of the world; it was nine leagues high. The protecting deities of the universe took

flight, but the Future Buddha remained unmoved beneath the Tree. And the god then assailed him, seeking to break his concentration.

Whirlwind, rocks, thunder and flame, smoking weapons with keen edges, burning coals, hot ashes, boiling mud, blistering sands and fourfold darkness, the Antagonist hurled against the Savior, but the missiles were all transformed into celestial flowers and ointments by the power of Gautama's ten perfections. Mara then deployed his daughters, Desire, Pining and Lust, surrounded by voluptuous attendants, but the mind of the Great Being was not distracted. (p. 32)

Anyone who has tried to meditate can identify with the difficulties that the Buddha faced, since they represent in metaphoric terms the ego's attempts to interfere with our concentration.

The universality of myths allows us to move beyond just personal reflection to a more contemplative state. Myths are filled with images that act in the same synthesizing manner as visualization; in short, they allow us to connect conscious and unconscious experience. As well, when individuals embed their stories into a larger story, they then belong to a timeless community of those who have traveled the path of transformation (Larsen, 1990).

SUMMARY

Meditation and myth are just two ways of moving toward contemplative practice. Several other modes are described in chapters 4 and 7. We now turn to the cosmological foundations of contemplation –the invisible world.

REFERENCES

Aquinas, Thomas. (1966). *Summa theologiae*. Vol. 46, *Action and contemplation*. Ed. J. Aumann. New York: Blackfriars.
Bernstein, R. J. (1976). *The restructuring of social and political theory*. New York: Harcourt Brace Jovanovich.

Buchman, M. (1989). The careful vision: How practical is contemplation in teaching? *American Journal of Education*, 78, 35-61.

Campbell, J. (1949). *The hero with a thousand faces*. Princeton, NJ: Princeton University Press.

——. (1988). *The power of myth*. New York: Doubleday.

Carrington, Patricia. (1977). *Freedom in meditation*. Garden City, NY: Anchor Press/Doubleday.

Deshimaru, T. (1985). *Questions to a Zen master*. New York: Dutton.

Emerson, R. W. (1965). *Selected writings*. New York: New American Library.

Erdman, J. (1987). Reflecting on teaching and adult education. *Lifelong Learning*, 10(8), 19-22.

Freedman, S. G. (1990). *Small victories: The real world of a teacher, her students and their high school*. New York: Harper & Row.

Fullan, M. & Connelly, F. (1987). *Teacher education in Ontario: Current practice and options for the future*. Ottawa, ON: Ministry of Education

Greene, M. (1987, Autumn). Sense making through story: An autobiographical inquiry. *Teaching Education*, 2, 9-14.

Greenwood, D. (1966). Attributes of a profession. In Vollmer and Mills (eds.), *Professionalization*. Englewood Cliffs, NJ: Prentice Hall.

Griffin, R. (1977, February). Discipline: What's it taking out of you? *Learning*, pp. 78-80.

Holmes Group. (1990). *Tomorrow's schools: Principles for the design of professional development schools*. East Lansing, MI: Author.

Larsen, S. (1990). *The mythic imagination*. New York: Bantam.

Lesh, T. V. (1970). Zen meditation and the development of empathy in counselors. *Journal of Humanistic Psychology*, 10, pp. 39-74.

Macrorie, K. (1984). *20 Teachers*. New York: Oxford University Press.

Merton, T. (1959). *The inner experience*. Unpublished manuscript. (Four drafts at Thomas Merton Studies Centre, Louisville, KY)

Miller, J. p. (1988). *The holistic curriculum*. Toronto: OISE Press.

Miller, R. (1988). The quest for vision: An interview with Joseph Jastrab. *Holistic Education Review*, 1(3), pp. 40-43.

Polanyi, M. (1962). *Personal knowledge: Towards a post-critical philosophy*. Chicago: University of Chicago Press.

Schein, E. (1973). *Professional education*. New York: McGraw-Hill.

Schon, D. A. (1983). *The reflective practitioner: How professionals think in action*. New York: Basic.

Teilhard de Chardin, p. (1965). *The phenomenon of man*. New York: Harper/Torch.

Trungpa, C. (1984). *Shambhala: The sacred path of the warrior*. Boston: Shambhala.

Vaughan, F. (1979). *Awakening intuition*. Garden City, NY: Anchor.

Wear, D. (1990). A pedagogy of bliss. *The Educational Forum*, 54 (3), pp. 283-291.

Wilber, K. (1983). *Eye to eye: The quest for the new paradigm*. Garden City, NY: Anchor Press/Doubleday.

3

The Invisible World

*Crazy Horse dreamed and went into the world where
there is nothing but the spirit of all things. That is the
real world that is behind this one, and everything we see
here is something like a shadow from that world.*

—Black Elk

For centuries across cultures, people have sensed a vaster reality
beyond the physical. Lao-tzu called this dimension the Tao, Plato
referred to it as the invisible world, Jung described it as the collective
unconscious, and David Bohm, the physicist, called it the implicate
order. Despite this long tradition, modern-day reality is rooted in
materialism and gives little credence or possibility to the invisible
world. Yet, now there are signs of awakening to this non-visible world.
Today, for example, there is great interest in the cosmologies of
indigenous peoples, which almost always include references to the
spirit realm.

Why should we be interested in the non-visible world? First, creative people throughout the centuries have gathered inspiration from
this world through the muse. The invisible world has been seen as a
primary source of creativity by both artists and scientists. Einstein
(1984) said, "The most beautiful experience we can have is the mysterious. It is the fundamental emotion which stands at the cradle of true
art and true science. . . . I am satisfied with the mystery of the eternity
of life" (p. 40). Second, for many individuals, through various experiences such as near-death, the invisible is associated with something very
nourishing and transforming. People who claim contact with the invis-

ible world speak of being in the presence of a great harmonious energy that sustains them in their daily life. The research on the effects of near-death experience is one example of these data (Moody, 1988). People who have practiced meditation for many years also can sense this non-visible world, and feel that it nourishes their inner life. Finally, many people see the non-visible reality as part of the order of the universe. It makes sense to people of many different traditions that there is this non-visible world that interconnects with the physical world. Emanuel Swedenborg, the Swedish mystic, believed that there is a correspondence between the physical and the spiritual world and that the former is somehow a mirror of the latter. Swedenborg's view is similar to Black Elk's, and provides a picture of the universe of multi-leveled realities.

Singer (1990) summarizes the influence of the non-visible world:

> It [the non-visible world] affects us profoundly through subliminal messages, feeling tones, unconscious impulses and reactions, hopes and dreams, fears and specters, and glimpses into the sometimes frightening, sometimes glorious realms of possibilities. The invisible world is also the one from which inspiration comes, in which new connections may be seen, and where we can sense the relatedness of all that appears to be separate and distinct in the visible world. (p. 2)

In this chapter I describe different conceptions of the non-visible world. I proceed chronologically with the descriptions and finish with the views of David Bohm as well as the views of indigenous and tribal societies, which are in a sense timeless. Of course, there are differences in these conceptions that reflect the social-cultural views of the individuals involved; however, it is apparent that these descriptions are attempting to portray the same realm. One of the problems is that these portrayals are attempting to describe what is indescribable; yet I believe that it is important to attempt the description, since despite wide differences in time and place, the continuity among the various conceptions is revealing. It is also helpful to view these descriptions as broad metaphors for the invisible world and avoid literal descriptions and interpretations. These descriptions point to a reality rather than describe it.

THE TAO

The Tao is described in the book *Tao Te Ching* by Lao-tzu. We know little about Lao-tzu except that he lived in China from 551 to 479 B.C. and may have been an archivist in one of the small kingdoms there. Stephen Mitchell (in Lao-tzu, 1988) summarizes Lao-tzu's contribution: "Like an Iroquois woodsman, he left no traces. All he left us is his book: the classic manual on the art of living, written in a style of gem-like lucidity, radiant with humor and grace and largeheartedness and deep wisdom: one of the wonders of the world" (p. vii).

Lao-tzu (1988) describes how each person can come in harmony with the Tao, or the way. The Tao is the larger unnameable reality of which we are a part. It is described as:

> The Tao is nowhere to be found.
> Yet it nourishes and completes all things. (p. 41)

Although we cannot see the Tao, or the invisible world, Lao-tzu suggests it nourishes and sustains all things. The Tao, then, is the primary source. This is important in most teachings regarding the invisible world: the non-visible world is primary and the physical world is secondary. If we lose this sense of order, suffering arises. If we assign to the physical world the primary reality, we end up grasping and holding on to physical things. Unfortunately, the physical world is transitory and subject to decay; our attempt to control it or make it permanent is futile and thus a source of much suffering. On the other hand, Tao, or the invisible world, is "Unchanging. Infinite. Eternally Present" (Lao-tzu, p. 25).

Lao-tzu (1988) also writes: "It [the Tao] is always present within you" (p. 6). This teaching is fundamental to all sacred traditions, as the invisible world is not separate from us or outside us. As Jesus said, "The Kingdom of God is within"; so the Tao resides in our own hearts. Our journey, or task, is to allow that which is within us to manifest itself. Unfortunately, our ego fears the Tao and struggles to maintain a sense of separateness from it. Today it seems modern civilization has lost touch with the way. Lao-tzu's words are prophetic.

> When man interferes with the Tao,
> the sky becomes filthy,
> the earth becomes depleted,
> the equilibrium crumbles,

creatures become extinct. (1988, p. 39)

Lao-tzu is very explicit about the principle that if we can be in harmony with the Tao then we will be "perfectly fulfilled" (p. 7). Although we cannot see or hear the Tao, Lao-tzu claims that "when you use it, it is inexhaustible" (p. 35). We can't use it up, for the Tao is an infinite source of energy.

Most of the *Tao Te Ching* discusses how we can live more in harmony with the Tao. The guidelines offered apply to all areas of life, including governing, social activity, and family life. By being in harmony with the Tao, we find that peace and fulfillment arise spontaneously in our lives.

PLATO

At the end of Book 6 in the *Republic*, Plato makes the distinction between the visible and the intelligible worlds. The latter is actually invisible. Each world requires its own set of habits. De Nicolas (1989) suggests that

> Plato's whole educational enterprise is concerned with developing quality in the performance of our inner acts. It is in relation to this quality of performance that he is able to sort out different worlds and the claims of the members of his community. These inner acts performed through education and training rely on their similarity to an original, invisible form. (p. 43)

After Plato introduces the dividing line, he then describes the famous allegory of the cave. In the cave prisoners are chained and see only shadows of themselves on the walls of the cave. The prisoners believe that these shadows are real. One prisoner is compelled to free himself, and he sees the fire which is the source of the shadows on the wall. He also is forced to climb up the ascent and leaves the cave to go outside, where he sees objects that are much clearer and more distinct. He also sees that the sun is the source of light as the fire was in the cave. He remembers the fate of his fellow prisoners and returns to teach them about what he has seen and learned. However, they are not ready for this wisdom and, like Socrates, the prisoner-teacher is killed by his fellow prisoners.

It is possible to see the cave and its shadows as the visible world of ordinary existence. The chains of the prisoner represent the limitations of time-space, and perception in the cave is ordinary sense perception. The escape from the cave represents the spiritual and philosophic quest for wisdom. The objects outside the cave can be seen as representing Plato's "Ideas or eternal Forms, whose reality and permanence transcend by far those of the physical world" (Capaldi, Kelly, & Navia, 1981, p. 69). The sun is the "Idea of the Good," which represents ultimate reality for Plato, who calls it "the universal author of things beautiful and right, parent of light and the lord of light in this visible world and the immediate source of reason and truth in the intellectual" (cited in Capaldi, Kelly, & Navia, p. 69). To come in contact with the sun is in some way a mystical experience, which then must be translated into reason. For Plato philosophy itself involves a strong spiritual element. Plato wrote a letter to his friend Dionysius (the king of Syracuse) about the problems of systematically representing his work. He avoided a systematic presentation of his thought because

> there is no way of putting it in words like other studies. Acquaintance with it must come rather after a long period of attendance on instruction in the subject itself and of close companionship, when, suddenly, like a blaze kindled by a leaping spark, it is generated in the soul and at once becomes self-sustaining. (Cited in Capaldi, Kelly, & Navia, p. 60)

Returning to the two worlds, the visible is perceptible but transitory. On the other hand, the invisible world is intelligible and eternal, and physical reality mirrors the world of Forms or Ideas. In other words, the table in the real world corresponds to the Idea of the table. This is similar to Swedenborg's notion of correspondence between physical and material reality. One problem with Plato's invisible world is that it appears static. Unlike the Tao, which contains infinite possibilities, Plato's invisible world seems rigid to many people.

To come in contact with the invisible world, Plato suggests various contemplative practices. For example, in the *Phaedo* 67c-d and in 79c-81a he talks about creating the "experience after death," or of achieving experience "through practicing death" by accustoming the soul to "withdraw from all contact with body and concentrate itself on itself alone by itself." (Cited in de Nicolas, 1989, p. 46)

To access the invisible world, we need different ways of knowing from those that we use in the physical world. De Nicolas (1989) describes these as habits of mind and offers an interesting educational program to develop these habits.

DANTE

In *The Divine Comedy*, Dante has drawn an elaborate picture of the invisible world; it is depicted as a journey from hell to heaven. This journey can be seen as a journey within ourselves where we finally awaken to a deeper wholeness and connectedness with the invisible world. In Dante's vision, there is no separation between our inner world and the invisible world.

Dante's journey starts in hell. Fortunately, Dante has been sent a guide, the poet Virgil, by his beloved Beatrice. Virgil, who represents reason, wisely guides Dante through hell and purgatory. Hell is a place where love is absent and the individuals there are caught deeply in self-deception. Honesty is essential to spiritual growth, and Dante has placed those who are dishonest in the lowest pit in the Inferno. In an age where we constantly question the credibility of our leaders, Dante's vision is a painful reminder of the spiritual morass of our age.

In purgatory individuals experience for the first time a sense of personal responsibility. People in purgatory have an urgent sense of time. Here people learn that growth and wholeness arise from attention. Helen Luke (1989) comments:

> The souls are unwilling to waste one moment of the daylight in spite of their great pleasure in talking to Dante. It is a point which awakens us to a truth so easily forgotten in this age–the truth that the way of individuation demands *attention,* not just for a few hours or weeks, or a few minutes a day, but ultimately, during every moment of our lives. . . . The experience of immortality will spring ultimately from constant attention to the "minute particular," in Blake's phrase. The point lies not in *what* we do, as the Puritans mistakenly defined this truth, but in the degree of our conscious awareness of every act and every impulse in their contexts outer and inner. True spontaneity is born of this awareness alone. (pp. 52-53)

Contemplation is a constant theme throughout *The Divine Comedy*. It is the attention, or the quality of consciousness, that we bring to each daily act that allows a gradual sense of connectedness to the invisible world to evolve within ourselves. In purgatory humans begin to learn to contemplate, which is in fact to pay attention. Near the end of Dante's journey in purgatory, Virgil leaves Dante so that Beatrice may guide him through paradise.

In paradise Dante comes in contact with the joy and bliss of the invisible world. For thirty-three cantos, Dante describes his vision of heaven. Again, this is an inner heaven as well as a depiction of the invisible world. Like the Tao, Dante's invisible world is a sustaining source, and is called the "bread of angels." Dante finds this bread through self-acceptance. Near the end of his journey, Dante fully accepts himself and does this with joy. Joy and heaven are often linked, but Dante has made the connection through complete forgiveness. As we immerse ourselves more deeply in the invisible realm, we feel more deeply both compassion and bliss.

Dante's journey through paradise involves travel to the planets. The last and highest of the planets that Dante visits is Saturn, where the souls of contemplatives reside. As noted earlier, attention and contemplation are fundamental to Dante's vision. Through contemplation the individual soul immerses itself more fully in the invisible world. Beatrice, his guide in paradise, says to Dante that through attention and witnessing we gradually are able to encompass a deeper joy. It is by witnessing, seeing, and contemplating that we gain the ability to experience true bliss. Beatrice states that light from God surrounds her and connects with her own sight and being. This light is similar to Plato's sun, which is the primary source of light and understanding. Both Dante and Plato also acknowledge that we can only access this source through some form of contemplation; reason or analysis will simply not be enough.

At the end of *The Divine Comedy* (1984), Dante comes to his final vision. The last line refers to "the Love that moves the sun and the other stars" (Canto 33, 140-145). Here Dante fully grasps that love is the animating principle of the universe. Dante saw the invisible world as Conscious Love, which expresses itself through the form of the physical world (e.g., the sun and the other stars).

SWEDENBORG

Emanuel Swedenborg (1688-1772) was the Swedish scientist-mystic who at midlife had a spiritual vision. His work has since influenced a variety of fields, such as religion, philosophy, homeopathy, architecture, poetry, and art. The impact of his work is best seen in the book *Emanuel Swedenborg: A Continuing Vision*, edited by Robin Larsen (1988).

Central to this vision is the concept of correspondence. For Swedenborg, the divine, or the source of all, works most directly through the spiritual realm (the invisible world) and also through the physical world (the visible), although its appearance is dimmed as the material world becomes denser. Like Plato, Swedenborg sees objects and events in the physical world as the result of images and ideas in the spiritual world. Larsen (1988) states:

> Swedenborg's original notion of correspondences, later more fully developed as a theory in his theological period, holds that nature is the symbolic manifestation of spirit or psyche. The world as we experience it is but a shadow of inconceivable spiritual realities, which it nonetheless prefigures in its intricacies and vital creativity.
>
> The realities hover next to each other, an existential hair's breadth apart, what he calls a "discrete degree." (p. 492)

William Blake, the English poet-artist, was deeply influenced by Swedenborg, and poetically encapsulates the idea of correspondence in the following lines:

> To see the world in a grain of sand,
> And heaven in a wild flower;
> Hold infinity in the palm of your hand,
> And eternity in an hour. (Cited in Larsen, 1988, p. 492)

Swedenborg, like other mystics, saw the physical reality as a microcosm of a much vaster spiritual reality (the macrocosm). Michael Talbot (1991) has made the connection between Swedenborg's thought and Bohm's holographic paradigm. Bohm's theory will be discussed later in this chapter. In brief, Bohm suggests that the physical world, or what he calls the explicate order, is connected to a deeper reality—the implicate order—which is an unbroken whole. Swedenborg saw the spiritual reality (Bohm's implicate order) as indivisible. Swedenborg (1915) stated: "In heaven no one can pronounce a trinity of persons each of whom separately is God—the heavenly aura itself, in which their thoughts fly and undulate the way sound does in our air, resists [such pronouncement]" (p. 173). For Swedenborg (1905-10), everything is connected: "Nothing unconnected ever occurs, and anything unconnected would instantly perish" (p. 2556).

For Swedenborg, like Dante, the ultimate reality is love (Hite, 1988). Hite concludes:

> Love exhibits the character of an infinity of infinities. Among such infinities are the animal and plant series; also such series as the rational and moral life. It is as member of such series and as constituting such series, that the individual is a proper function of the universe, and is related to the universe as a whole. (p. 415)

As we immerse ourselves in the spiritual reality, we experience love. Love is an ultimate form of connectedness where all separateness is viewed as illusion.

Swedenborg's (1979) description of spiritual reality in his book *Heaven and Hell* is detailed, and some find all the details hard to accept. Yet it is difficult to deny the power of Swedenborg's vision and its parallels with other portrayals of the invisible world.

EMERSON

Swedenborg was one of the many thinkers who influenced the American transcendentalist Ralph Waldo Emerson. Although influenced by many thinkers, Emerson (1968) developed his own unique vision. He called the invisible the Over-Soul. The Over-Soul is

> that great nature in which we rest as the earth lies in the soft arms of the atmosphere; that Unity, that Over-Soul, within which every man's particular being is contained and made one with all other; that common heart of which all sincere conversation is the worship,

> to which all right action is submission; that overpower-
> ing reality which confutes our tricks and talents, and
> constrains every one to pass for what he is and to
> speak from his character and not from his tongue, and
> which evermore tends to pass into our thought and
> hand and become wisdom and virtue and power and
> beauty. (p. 262)

The Over-Soul, like the Tao, is a source of "wisdom and virtue
and power and beauty." Emerson sees the line between the physical
and spiritual as a very thin one. He says the Over-Soul is "undefinable,
unmeasurable; but we know that it pervades and contains us. We know
that all spiritual being is in man. . . . [T]here is no screen or ceiling
between our heads and the infinite heavens, so is there no bar or wall in
the soul, where man, the effect, ceases and God, the cause, begins" (p.
264). Emerson suggests that we can come in contact with the invisible
through contemplation, which "redeems us in a degree from the
conditions of time" (p. 264). If we can simply let the Over-Soul act
through us, then we know the right thing to do. Emerson closes his
essay on the Over-Soul with a vision similar to those of Swedenborg
and Blake.

> Thus revering the soul, and learning, as the ancient said,
> that "its beauty is immense," man will come to see that
> the world is the perennial miracle which the soul
> worketh, and be less astonished at particular wonders; he
> will learn that here is no profane history; that all history
> is sacred; that the universe is represented in an atom in a
> moment of time; he will weave no longer a spotted life
> of shreds and patches, but will live with a divine unity.
> He will cease from what is base and frivolous in his life
> and be content with all places and with any service he
> can render. He will calmly front the morrow in the
> negligency of that trust which carries God with it and so
> hath already the whole future in the bottom of the heart.
> (p. 278)

By coming in contact with the invisible world, we answer wholeheart-
edly in the affirmative Einstein's fundamental question: Is the universe
friendly?

JUNG

Carl Jung, the Swiss psychologist, at the end of *Memories, Dreams, Reflections* (1961) wrote,

> The decisive question for man is, is he related to something infinite or not? That is the telling question of his life. Only if we know that the thing that truly matters is the infinite can we avoid fixing our attention upon futilities and upon all kinds of goals which are not of real importance. . . . In the final analysis we count for something only because of the essential we embody, and if we do not embody that, life is wasted. (p. 325)

Jung's conception of the infinite lay in his notion of the collective unconscious. Collective unconscious is to culture what personal unconsciousness is to personal ego. It is the vast, yes, infinite, realm of possibility. Singer (1990) comments on the collective unconscious:

> On the far side [of the collective unconscious] is the unknowable–that is, unknowable by any rational means. If it can be known at all, it has to be through a process of subjective knowing. That means that it comes to one person at a time, in a way unique to that person, and that it cannot be validated by any of the methods that are culturally approved in the rational, visible world. (p. 43)

One way that we can access the collective unconscious is through archetypes. Archetypes are symbols that represent universal or culturally specific themes. Often the archetype is an image that becomes predominant in one's life. For example, the Hero archetype encourages the adolescent to move away from the Great Mother archetype (Feinstein & Krippner, 1988). Archetypes can follow one another in one's life as different themes emerge. Symbols from nature such as the sun and water are universal archetypes. The archetype can be compared to Plato's Idea or Form in that they exist in the invisible world in the pure form and are manifested in various ways in the physical world.

Archetypes can be accessed as vehicles for personal integration. In psychosynthesis, there are various guided imagery activities that use symbols such as the rose to facilitate wholeness and connectedness.

Sometimes spontaneous images emerge in meditation or daily life that deepen one's connection to the invisible world. Jung saw these images as arising from the Self, or the collective unconsciousness, and as extremely important to the individuation of the person.

Singer (1990) also draws a comparison between Jung's collective unconscious and Bohm's implicate order. She writes. "For Jung, the collective unconscious was the fundamental reality, with human consciousness deriving from it. In a similar way, Bohm sees the implicate order as the fundamental reality with the explicate order and all its manifestations as derivative" (p. 66). Again, the collective unconscious (the invisible world) is seen as primary and the physical reality as secondary.

BOHM

David Bohm (1980) is a physicist who has developed a theory that the universe is like a hologram. A hologram is a three-dimensional image that is produced when a single laser light is split into two different beams. One beam is reflected off an object, while the second beam collides with the reflected beam to form an interference pattern that is recorded on the film. What is particularly interesting about the pattern on the film is that any piece of the film will contain the image of the object. Holography, then, reflects the principle that has been outlined by Swedenborg that the microcosm reflects the macrocosm.

Bohm has argued that the hologram can explain some of the unusual behavior seen in subatomic physics. Physicists refer to the behavior of some subatomic particles as nonlocal, that is, they don't behave according to the normal laws of time and space. For example, two particles that seem unconnected and are not physically close to one another seem to move in common patterns. Bohm explains this behavior through his concept of enfolded (implicate) and unfolded (explicate) orders. The implicate order is the non-visible world that lies behind the explicate order and is a deeply interconnected whole.

The example of implicate and explicate orders is found in Bohm's example of a jar full of glycerine in which a drop of ink is placed. If we stir the jar, then the ink disappears (e.g., it becomes enfolded). However, if we stir in the opposite direction, then the ink will appear (e.g., it becomes unfolded). The whole, however, is not static. Bohm has introduced the concept of holomovement in an attempt to portray the dynamism of the universe. Each particular object or event that we see as separate is actually part of this holomovement. Although we see each object and event as separate, these events and objects are part of a whole.

Bohm's work has also been connected with the research of Karl Pibram, who argues that the brain is like a hologram. Taking the work of Pibram and Bohm together, Talbot (1991) says: "Our brains mathematically construct objective reality by interpreting frequencies that are ultimately projections from another dimension, a deeper order of existence that is beyond both space and time: The brain is a hologram enfolded in a holographic universe" (p. 54).

Bohm (Bohm & Weber, 1982) himself has speculated that his implicate order is like the invisible world of the mystic. In an interview, he stated that the implicate order "could equally well be called Idealism, Spirit, Consciousness. The separation of the two–matter and spirit–is an abstraction. The ground is always one" (p. 40). Like Dante, he explored the importance of contemplation and attention in coming in contact with the invisible world. Bohm reflects: "At the present, our whole thought process is telling us that we have to keep our attention here. . . . Contact with eternity is in the present moment, but it is mediated by thought. It is a matter of attention" (cited in Talbot, 1991, p. 261).

The way to the invisible world, as explained by Dante and Bohm, is through careful attention to the here and now. Through conscious attention we are no longer bounded by ego-chatter and belief systems; instead, the universe and the invisible world are revealed to us. Michael Talbot (1991) has written a fascinating book about Bohm's theory entitled *The Holographic Universe*.

TRIBAL WISDOM

Talbot makes the connection between Bohm's holographic reality and the mystic or shamanistic thinking of indigenous peoples. Indigenous peoples see reality as deeply interconnected. The Hawaiian kahunas, for example, see everything as connected, and the shaman sees himself in the center of this interconnected web. Of course, within the web every point is a center. Talbot (1991) comments: "Like Bohm, who says that consciousness always has its source in the implicate, the aborigines believe that the true source of the mind is in the transcendent reality of the dreamtime" (p. 289). Dreamtime, another metaphor for the implicate order, is the primary reality that Crazy Horse refers to in the quote at the beginning of this chapter.

Douglas Sharon (1978) suggests that the concept of implicate and explicate orders can be found in most tribal traditions. He states: "Probably the central concept of shamanism, wherever in the world it is found, is the notion that underlying all the visible forms in the world, animate and inanimate, there exists a vital essence from which they emerge and by which they are nurtured. Ultimately everything returns to this ineffable, mysterious, impersonal unknown" (p. 49).

The shaman takes the drug so that he or she can come more directly in contact with the dream world. The journey into the spirit realm is like a pilgrimage. The main reason for embarking on this pilgrimage is that the shaman is concerned about maintaining the balance between the physical world and the spirit world.

Sometimes the pilgrimage is actually a physical journey. For example, the Huichol Indians, who live in the Sierra Madre Occidental of central Mexico, make a sacred journey to Wirikuta, hundreds of miles from their own community. The Huichol Indians take this journey so that they can retrace the steps of their ancestors, and in doing so they actually come in contact with the realm that the ancestors inhabit. Maybury-Lewis (1992) claims that the "Huichols take this journey so that they can 'find their lives' after the manner of the Ancient Ones" (p. 224). The shaman gives them the drug peyote to enable them to enter into the spirit world. Some of the Huichols find this experience so powerful that they want to stay in paradise, which would mean death on the physical plane. The shaman must guide them so that they can return and bring their vision of the spirit world into daily life. Through this experience, the Huichols realize that the transitory existence on the physical plane is made whole by the mystical experience. According to Maybury-Lewis, "It is this knowledge that gives meaning to their lives and accounts for their insistence that the Huichol way of life is the most beautiful on earth" (p. 228).

Maybury-Lewis (1992) contrasts the experience of the tribal connection with the invisible world with our secular world:

> We live in a world that prides itself on its modernity, yet is hungry for wholeness, hungry for meaning. At the same time it is a world that marginalizes those very impulses that fill the void. The pilgrimage toward the divine, the openness to knowledge that transcends ordinary experience, the very idea of feeling at one with the

universe, these are impulses which we tolerate at the fringes, where they are held at bay by our indifference.

Shorn of the knowledge that we are part of something greater than ourselves, we lose also the sense of responsibility that comes with it. It is this connectedness that tribal societies cherish and that we cannot bring ourselves to seek. But if we do not listen to other traditions, do not even listen to our inner selves, then what will the future hold for our stunted and overconfident civilization? (pp. 231, 234)

SUMMARY

Maybury-Lewis's last question leads to the end of this chapter. What have we lost by ignoring the invisible world, and what can we realize by our acknowledgment of it?

One could argue, as Bohm and others have, that the major problems of today come from fragmentation and severing ourselves from the invisible world. Certainly environmental and social chaos are some of the results of this fragmentation. If we humans see ourselves as the summit of evolution entitled to use the earth for whatever ends we desire, then we will simply use it up. But the interconnectedness even of the physical world has come back to haunt us. The air we breathe and the water we drink are becoming foul. We realize that unless we reverse the process of environmental degradation, then we may die.

Our social chaos may also arise from not seeing that we are related to a larger spiritual reality. If in fact we arise and then pass back into a greater consciousness, we realize that we may meet the same difficulties after death that we face now. A larger spiritual reality means that there is no place to hide. This is not a last judgment or hellfire; it is simply what Emerson (1968) called the law of compensation. He said, "What we call retribution is the universal necessity by which the whole appears wherever a part appears" (p. 16). Today we have made a fetish of money and fame, while we ignore the larger reality that actually sustains us. This fundamental discontinuity has led to greed, violence, and chaos.

Our journey through various conceptions of the vision of the invisible world has led us to certain principles that might lead us out of our fragmentation. These principles include:

1. The invisible world is the primary reality. Physical reality arises from this primary reality and then passes back into it. Physical reality by definition is transitory, since all matter decays. The invisible, on the other hand, is eternal. Not only is it eternal, but it is characterized by an energy that Dante, Swedenborg, and other mystics identify as love. Love as the animating principle of the universe is a metaphor for the invisible world.

2. The invisible world nourishes and sustains us. In Emerson's words, it is the fount of "wisdom, virtue, power and beauty." Scientists and artists have also claimed that it is the primary source of inspiration.

3. The invisible world is not separate from the physical. The two are closely connected. It is possible to see physical reality as a microcosm of the larger reality, as depicted in the holographic view of reality.

4. The invisible world is not separate from us but lies within our own hearts. Various forms of spiritual practice involve awakening to this principle.

5. The way to access the invisible world is not through reason and analysis, but through various forms of contemplation. As Dante and others stress, contemplation can simply be the full attention that we bring to our daily acts.

Some of these principles are described by Jacques Lusseyran (1987). Lusseyran became blind at age 7 and was involved in the French Resistance during World War II. This activity led to his internment in a German concentration camp.

> Being blind I thought I should have to go out to meet things, but I found that they came to meet me instead. I have never had to go more than halfway, and the universe became the accomplice of all my wishes. . . .
>
> Touching the tomatoes in the garden, and really touching them, touching the walls of the house, the materials of the curtains or a clod of earth is surely seeing them as fully as eyes can see. But it is more than seeing them, it is tuning in on them and allowing the current they hold to connect with one's own, like electricity. To put it differently, this means an end of

living in front of things and the beginning of living with
them. Never mind if the word sounds shocking, for this
is love. (pp. 27-28)

Lusseyran describes so simply and vividly how to come in contact
with the invisible world. By touching things in a way that we connect
with the current within each object, we experience love at the most fundamental level.

By awakening to the invisible world, the healing process for the
earth and ourselves can begin. I believe this awakening has begun, as
evidenced in the deepening concern for the environment, interest in
tribal people's wisdom (Knudtson & Suzuki, 1992), and in many other
changes that are happening globally (Rifkin, 1991).

Probably the greatest insight of the twelve-step program that helps
alcoholics and others recover is that to heal ourselves we need to
acknowledge a power greater than ourselves. Unfortunately, organized
religion has fragmented this power and made it external to ourselves.
Ultimately, we must contact this power within our own hearts. Through
this act, we make the invisible world visible in our daily acts. By connecting the invisible with the visible, we start to realize a basic wholeness with ourselves and with the earth.

REFERENCES

Bohm, D. (1980). *Wholeness and the implicate order*. London:
    Routledge and Kegan Paul.
Bohm, D., & Weber, R. (1982). Nature as creativity. *Revision*, 5(2).
Capaldi, N., Kelly, E., & Navia, L. E. (1981). *An invitation to philoso-
    phy*. Buffalo, NY: Prometheus.
Dante, Alighieri. (1984). *Paradiso: The third book of the divine
    comedy*. Trans. A. Mandelbaum. New York: Bantam & Quality
    Paperback Book Club.
de Nicolas, A. (Ed.) (1989). *Habits of mind: An introduction to the
    philosophy of education*. New York: Paragon.
Einstein, A. (1984). *Einstein: A portrait*. Corte Madera, CA:
    Pomegranate Artbooks.
Emerson, R. W. (1968). *The selected writings of Ralph Waldo
    Emerson*. Ed. B. Atkinson. New York: Random House.
——. (1985). *The sage from Concord*. Wheaton, IL: Quest.

Feinstein, D., & Krippner, S. (1988). *Personal mythology: The psychology of your evolving self.* Los Angeles, CA: Jeremy p. Tarcher.

Hite, L. F. (1988). Love: The ultimate reality. In R. Larsen (ed.), *Emanuel Swedenborg: A continuing vision.* New York: Swedenborg Foundation

Jung, C. (1961). *Memories, dreams, reflections.* Ed. A. Jaffe. New York: Random House.

Knudtson, p., & Suzuki, D. (1992). *Wisdom of the elders.* Toronto: Stoddart.

Lao-tzu. (1988). *Tao te ching.* Ed. S. Mitchell. New York: Harper & Row.

Larsen, R. (Ed.) (1988). *Emanuel Swedenborg: A continuing vision.* New York: Swedenborg Foundation.

Luke, H. (1989). *Dark wood to white rose.* New York: Parabola.

Lusseyran, J. (1987). *And there was light.* New York: Parabola.

Maybury-Lewis, D. (1992). *Millenium: Tribal wisdom and the modern world.* New York: Viking.

Moody, R. (1988). *The light beyond.* New York: Bantam.

Neihardt, J. G. (1988). *Balck Elk speaks: Being the life story of a holy man of the Oglala Sioux.* Lincoln, NB: Univ. of Nebraska Press.

Rifkin, J. (1991). *Biosphere Politics.* New York: Crown.

Sharon, D. (1978). *Wizard of the four winds: A shaman's story.* New York: Free Press.

Singer, J. (1990). *Seeing though the visible world: Jung gnosis and chaos.* New York: Harper & Row.

Swedenborg, E. (1905-10). *Arcana coelestia.* Ed. J. F. Potts. New York: American Swedenborg Printing and Publishing Society.

——.(1915). *The true Christian religion.* Trans. J. Ager. New York: Swedenborg Foundation.

——. (1979). *Heaven and Hell.* Trans. and revised G. Dole. New York: Swedenborg Foundation.

Talbot, M. (1991). *The holographic universe.* New York: Harper.

4

Contemplative Practice: Meditation

In the West we tend to associate meditation with gurus and mysticism. This is unfortunate. Meditation is a simple practice that focuses on the development of attention.

We now have evidence that attention is profoundly healing. Dr. Gary Schwartz has done research that focuses on the importance of connectedness and attention (Kabat-Zinn, 1990, pp. 227-9). According to Schwartz, human beings are interconnected organisms that are self-regulating. Self-regulation refers to how mind and body interact to maintain our health. If the self-regulation breaks down through disconnection, then disorder or disease develops. Dr. Schwartz states that disattention, or not listening to the messages that our body sends to us, leads to disconnection and disease. If our heads are filled with thoughts, or our lives so rushed that we can't listen, then attention becomes very difficult. As a result, we don't hear messages from our body about what foods are appropriate or how much rest and exercise we need. Jon Kabat-Zinn (1990) summarizes this research when he says: "*Attention leads to connection; connection to regulation; regulation to order; and order to ease* (as opposed to dis-ease) *or more colloquially, to health.*" (p. 228)

Through meditation practice we attempt to develop a strength of attention that can carry through the day. Gradually, we begin to notice that we can focus more easily. One of my students who was studying for her comprehensive examination ("comps") put it this way:

> *My ability to concentrate on my work after meditating seems greater. Getting closer to "comps" and such, my*

ability to retain what I'm reading I feared was
diminishing. But today I noticed an alertness, an
attention to my work, which I began after meditating.

The attention we develop through meditation not only can help in
our work, but can enrich the little moments of the day. We seem to
become more aware of the beauty in nature and the joy of children at
play, and yes, more attuned to the suffering of others. Attention connects us more deeply with everything that is happening around us.

As indicated in the first chapter, there are physiological and psychological benefits to meditation. Murphy (1992) has recently summarized these benefits from over 1300 studies. Some of the benefits
include lowered heart rate, reduced blood pressure, heightened perception, increased empathy, anxiety reduction, relief from addiction, alle-
viation of pain, and improvements in memory and learning ability.
Meditation has also been linked to the reversal of heart disease. Along
with other changes such as improvements in diet and exercise, Dean
Ornish (1990) has found that meditation is an important factor in
reversing heart illness.

In related research, Redford Williams suggests that lifestyle
changes such as meditation are important to the development of the
"trusting heart." Williams (1989) found that what is particularly dam-
aging to the heart is hostility and anger. People who carry hostility are
more prone to heart attack than the average population. In contrast,
people who have trusting hearts have a much greater chance to be
healthy:

> The trusting heart believes in the basic goodness of
> humankind, that most people will be fair and kind in
> relationships with others. Having such beliefs, that
> trusting heart is slow to anger. Not seeking out evil in
> others, not expecting the worst of them, the trusting
> heart expects mainly good from others and, more often
> than not, finds it. As a result, the trusting heart spends
> little time feeling resentful, irritable, and angry.
>
> From this it follows that the trusting heart treats
> others well, with consideration and kindness; the trusting
> heart almost never wishes or visits harm upon others.
> Just as our research has shown that the hostile heart is at
> risk of premature death and disease, it also can reassure

us that the trusting heart appears protected against these outcomes. (Williams, 1989, p. 71)

To develop the trusting heart, Williams suggests a twelve-point program. Some of the recommendations are meditative in nature, for example:

- Monitor your cynical thoughts.
- Practice the relaxation response.
- Force yourself to listen more.
  (pp. 195-196)

Monitoring your thoughts is a form of meditation where we mindfully watch the thoughts as they arise. Meditation allows the individual to be less caught up in his or her thoughts through the process of compassionate awareness. The relaxation response, recommended by Herbert Benson, is actually a form of meditation in which the individual focuses his or her attention on repeating the number one. Finally, listening more is another form of meditation. Meditation can actually be described as "deep listening" during which we attune ourselves to what is happening within and outside.

Meditation allows us to feel more comfortable with ourselves and "at home" with the world around us. One of my students makes this point.

> *Now when I have difficulty at the beginning of the meditation, sometimes even into ten minutes or so, I just keep with it. I can now "work through" the initial difficulty of blocking out noises and tension. I now know what the benefits are if one perseveres. There is also a wonderful feeling of getting beyond the busyness and of feeling detached from the nonsense. It's giving me a new way for viewing my daily activities.*

Meditation also seems to facilitate the creative process. The meditative state is conducive to creativity because it promotes a relaxed state in which we are more open to new insights. There is also research that indicates that meditation facilitates productivity, quality, and stamina in relation to the creative process (Carrington, 1977, pp. 227-240). For example, increase in productivity depends on the ability of ideas to flow easily and rapidly. Meditation tends to bring about such a release of ideas.

There is also some evidence that meditation increases the quality of creative work as well. Artists, for example, have reported an improvement in the quality of their work as a result of meditation. With regard to stamina, meditation may facilitate increases in the overall energy level.

Meditation is not a cure-all. However, we do have enough evidence to suggest that it is useful in countering stress and in increasing our efficiency in day-to-day living. A final reason for practicing meditation relates to stages of adult development. Carl Jung suggests that after 35, an individual's basic concerns are of an inward nature. As the finiteness of life becomes more apparent, there is a tendency to be less concerned with the opinions of others and there is more focus on the inner life (LeShan, 1974, p. 172). Another way of putting this is that spiritual concerns become paramount after the age of 35. Carl Jung also stated that most psychological difficulties in those over 35 stemmed from spiritual concerns and that once these concerns were dealt with, then the psychological problems were usually resolved. Meditation, then, can be useful to the individual in dealing with this shift in concerns and can be an important key to adult growth and integration.

A MEDITATIVE STANCE

This chapter outlines several meditative techniques; however, before describing these it is important to discuss attitudes that help one approach meditative practice.

Openness

Each meditation is a new experience. If we approach each sitting as a fresh experience without preconceived expectations, we have already made significant progress in our meditation practice. If we come to each sitting with an open mind, then, we are already on the meditative path. However, if we come with a specific set of expectations for each sitting, we have already set up a model of what should happen. For example, if yesterday's meditation was peaceful and I find today's meditation filled with troubling thoughts, I have to let go of yesterday's experience. If I judge today's experience in relation to yesterday's meditation, I will make today's practice even more problematic than it actually is. Meditation involves releasing all models and expectations.

Release

Release, or letting go, is also fundamental to meditation practice. Our minds tend to cling to pleasure and to push away unpleasant thoughts. This clinging and pushing away is so fundamental to our thinking that we are hardly even aware of it. Yet, if we watch this grasping and pushing away, we realize how fatiguing it actually is. Why not simply release the attempts to cling to what we feel is pleasant? At a deeper level we can become aware that everything is changing and impermanent and our attempts to grasp and hold on are futile. If we approach meditation with an attitude of simply releasing what we can never really hold, then life and our meditation practice become much lighter. The heaviness comes from our grasping. We grasp for so much–material goods, pleasure–and we also attempt to control other people. To see meditation as a process of release is a major step on the meditative path.

Being, Not Doing

We are so task oriented in our lives. If we are not working, we feel that we must fill our lives with other activities so that we have "accomplished" something. Even in our leisure hours, we often feel hounded by the pressure to produce.

Meditation requires a different stance. It is not a task to be performed. Instead, we practice doing nothing. This is so hard for most of us. When I first tell my students that they will be doing some form of meditation in my class as a requirement, they often become quite upset. Their reaction frequently is: "How can you do this to me, I am a busy person, I don't have the time to just sit and do nothing." Gradually, however, most of my students end up looking forward to the meditation time, as they find it very nourishing and restoring. One of the reasons it is so nourishing is that we are not performing. We simply are. We begin to accept ourselves at a deeper level.

Acceptance

In meditation we gradually learn to accept all that happens. We don't push things away. Many thoughts, images, and feelings arise during meditation, and our first instinct is to push some of them away. For example, one of my students had worked with a friend who died of AIDS, and during her meditation images and memories from this experience came up. At first she was upset by this, as many of the thoughts and memories were painful. However, she wrote to me in her journal that after a while she realized the meditation was allowing her to accept the experience at a deeper level. If we are repressing something that has happened to us, sometimes meditation will allow us to work with it and integrate the experience. This acceptance leads to a sense of wholeness.

Big Mind, Long-Enduring Mind

There are certain metaphors regarding the mind that are helpful in approaching meditation practice. One metaphor is to see our minds as large, like the sky. If our minds are large, irritating thoughts and feelings are seen as rather insignificant. Thoughts, then, become like clouds that float by. When I am flying in an airplane, I love to look out and see the clear blue sky that stretches seemingly forever. It reminds me of the big mind. In contrast, if we see our minds as small and restricted, our thoughts have little room, and as a result, we can't let go of them. The thoughts take over.

Also helpful is the notion of the long-enduring mind. The long-enduring mind is the patient mind that can wait and deal with all that arises. The long-enduring mind knows that what arises eventually passes away. In our culture, we tend to focus on the short term, whether it be profits or test results. It would be wiser to take the longer-term view. With the longer-term view, we watch things from a bigger perspective, and thus we do not "react" all the time. We are not constantly weighing and reacting to everything that happens to us. When we are constantly reacting, we become agitated and tired. The long-enduring mind is a mind at peace.

Grace

Grace is a term not often associated with meditation practice, particularly when we use a meditation approach based on Eastern spiritual practice. However, I believe it is helpful to see meditation as a grace, or gift. We must have a certain level of comfort and leisure to do meditation. People who are struggling to survive from day to day usually cannot meditate. In this sense, we can approach meditation as a gift, since we have been presented with circumstances in our life that enable us to do the practice. Approaching meditation with an attitude of grace means that we are simply thankful for the opportunity to see ourselves and the world around us in a clearer light.

The other aspect of grace is that at some level we can acknowledge that meditation allows us to be connected to something larger than ourselves. Whether we call this something God, Christ, Krishna, or Buddha is not the issue. Meditation can let us feel a part of something that, although unseen, is quite wonderful. This is the invisible world, the world described earlier in this book as a realm that is immensely nourishing and sustaining. To be in contact with that world even for a moment is an act of grace.

When we approach meditation, it is not so important that we keep all these points in mind. To be rather mundane, the important thing is to "just do it." If we simply approach meditation with an openness, everything just takes care of itself; a process unfolds. We don't have to believe anything, we just need to watch. Of course, teachings can be helpful in the process. To approach meditation or any spiritual practice, we don't abandon natural skepticism. I know about natural skepticism, since I come from the "show me" state, Missouri. Natural skepticism is not cynicism but simply testing what we hear or read against our experience and common sense. We need to avoid embracing meditation or any spiritual practice as *the* answer. Meditation is a method or practice; it helps us along our journey, but there is much more to the journey than meditation.

FORMS OF MEDITATION

When beginning meditation practice, it is helpful to pick a method you feel comfortable with. It is possible to categorize approaches to meditation according to four different types: intellectual, emotional, physical, and action-service.

Intellectual approaches to meditation focus on awareness and discrimination. Meditation is seen as a form of inquiry into the mind-body process. This is not inquiry as problem solving as we traditionally use the term in the West; instead, meditative inquiry is a deeper form of inquiry into the basic processes of life. Insight, or vipassana meditation, which comes from the teachings of the Buddha, can be looked at in this light. Krishnamurti also practiced this form of meditative inquiry. He would take a question and then explore it completely. For example, Krishnamurti (1963) was asked the question, How is one to be intelligent?

> What is implied in this question? You want a method by which to be intelligent—which implies that you know what intelligence is. When you want to go some place, you already know your destination and you only have to ask the way. Similarly, you think you know what intelligence is, and you want a method by which you can be intelligent. Intelligence is the very questioning of the method. Fear destroys intelligence, does it not? Fear prevents you from examining, questioning, inquiring; it prevents you from finding out what is true. Probably you will be intelligent when there is no fear. So you have to inquire into the whole question of fear, and be free of fear; and then there is the possibility of your being intelligent. But if you say, "How am I to be intelligent?" you are merely cultivating a method, and so you become stupid. (p. 40)

Emotional forms of meditation connect with the heart. Mantra meditation, which involves repeating a phrase or word over and over again, tends to be emotionally oriented. One of the classic mantras is the Jesus prayer: "Lord Jesus, Son of God, have mercy on me." *The Way of the Pilgrim*, a classic in spiritual literature, describes how a Russian monk traveling in Russia constantly repeated the Jesus prayer and how this process transformed him and those that he came in contact with. In the Hindu religion, the devotee recites the name of God, Ram, over and over again.

Physical meditation involves various forms of movement. Hatha yoga, tai chi, akido, and the martial arts are movement meditations. The practitioner is deeply attentive to the physical movement. This type of meditation may appeal to people who are athletically oriented. The following story is an example of the physical approach to meditation:

> There is the Hasidic tale of the great Rabbi who was coming to visit a small town in Russia. It was a very great event for the Jews in the town and each thought long and hard about what questions they would ask the wise man. When he finally arrived, all were gathered in the largest available room and each was deeply concerned with the questions they had for him. The Rabbi came into the room and felt the great tension in it. For a time he said nothing and then began to hum softly a Hasidic tune. Presently all there were humming with him. He then began to sing the song and soon all were singing with him. Then he began to dance and soon all present were caught up in the dance with him. After a time all were deeply involved in the dance, all fully committed to it, all just dancing and nothing else. In this way, each one became whole with himself, each healed the splits within himself which kept him from understanding. After the dance went on for a time, the Rabbi gradually slowed it to a stop, looked at the group, and said, "I trust that I have answered all your questions." (LeShan, 1974, pp. 50-51)

Action meditation is service oriented. One works in the world with the idea that each act is an offering to the divine. The work of Mother Theresa can be seen in this light. The action is not viewed as a way of improving or changing the world. Instead the action is performed in a way that lets us deepen our relationship with God.

The world is seen as a vast schoolroom where we are presented with what we need to learn at each moment in our lives. In Hinduism this is called karma yoga. Huston Smith (1986) describes the basic approach:

> The world is the soul's gymnasium, its school, its training field. What we do is important, but ultimately it is important for the discipline it offers our individual spirits; we delude ourselves if we expect it to change the world in any fundamental way. Our work in this world is like bowling in an uphill alley; it can develop nice muscles, but we should not think that by our throws the

balls are transported to the other end in any permanent way. They all roll back eventually to confront our children if we happen to have moved along. The world can develop character and teach men to look beyond it—for these it is admirably suited—but it can never be converted into a paradise in which man is fully at home. "Said Jesus, blessed be his name, this world is a bridge: pass over it, but build no house upon it." (p. 108)

MEDITATIONS

Insight

Insight, or vipassana, meditation focuses on being aware of what happens in each moment. This meditation usually starts with an awareness of the flow of the breath. One simply follows either the breath coming in and out of the nostrils or the rising and falling of the abdomen. The eyes are usually closed and we may label the flow of the breath with "in and out" if following the breath in the nostrils, or "rising and falling" if following the movement of the abdomen. Insight meditation, however, does not stay with the breath as the sole focus. Although it is the anchor to which we can always return, the awareness gradually moves to other phenomena. For example, the awareness can also focus on the sensations that may arise in the body. If our knee starts to hurt, or our arm itches, the attention can shift to these sensations. The mind simply notices these sensations as they arise, stays focused on them, and then notices them passing away. The term "insight" is based, to a large extent, on this watching of the arising and passing away of phenomena.

Another area that we can focus on is feelings, which also may arise during meditation. For example, if we have had an argument with our spouse, we might be filled with feelings of anger. These feelings are sometimes so powerful that they take over, and we lose our basic awareness of what is happening. In this case we can come back to the breath to gain our balance, and then return to an awareness of the anger. Insight can also come from witnessing that we are not the anger that arises and then passes away. Yes, there are these feelings, but because they are impermanent, we gain the understanding that we don't have to identify or to become the feeling.

Another area of focus is our thoughts. Our mind is filled with thoughts, and we can also be taken over by these. For example, thoughts relating to our work can be quite strong, and during our meditation we simply try to stay aware of these thoughts. One technique for watching our thoughts is to see them as clouds floating by. Another technique is to label the thoughts. At a general level we can label all thoughts as "thinking," or we can be more specific and label the nature of the thoughts. For example, we can use labels like planning, remembering, or imagining. Suzuki Roshi gives some helpful advice on observing our thoughts. They relate to the metaphor of "big mind" discussed earlier.

> When you are practicing Zazen meditation do not try to stop your thinking. Let it stop by itself. If something comes into your mind, let it come in and let it go out. It will not stay long. When you try to stop your thinking, it means you are bothered by it. Do not be bothered by anything. It appears that the something comes from outside your mind, but actually it is only the waves of your mind and if you are not bothered by the waves, gradually they will become calmer and calmer. . . . If you leave your mind as it is, it will become calm. This mind is called big mind. (Cited in Goldstein, 1976, p. 28)

Another focus for the insight process is sound. If any sound arises, then our attention turns to the sound. If a car passes outside or someone turns on the television in the next apartment, we notice the sound and then return to the breathing again as our anchor.

Eventually with insight meditation, our attention shifts to whatever is predominant in the moment. For example, if my back is sore, my attention shifts to the soreness. If my thoughts start to react to the pain, I notice these thoughts. If any related feelings arise, I notice these feelings. If my mind becomes too unsettled by all this, I simply return to the breath. Gradually, however, this meditation allows me to live in the present moment. It allows our natural awareness to arise, so that we are not encumbered by our thoughts and feelings. We experience more fully each moment rather than living in the past or projecting ourselves into the future. We gradually learn that all we really have to experience is what is happening right now.

One of the best books on insight meditation is Joseph Goldstein's *The Experience of Insight: A Natural Unfolding*. In this book, Goldstein (1976) says:

> Just let things happen as they do. Let all images and
> thoughts and sensations rise and pass away without
> being bothered, without reacting, without judging,
> without clinging, without identifying with them.
> Become one with the big mind, observing carefully,
> microscopically, all the waves coming and going. This
> attitude will quickly bring about a state of balance and
> calm. Don't let the mind get out of focus. Keep the
> mind sharply aware, moment to moment, of what is
> happening, whether the in-out breath, the rising-falling,
> sensations, or thoughts. In each instant be focused on
> the object with a balanced and relaxed mind. (p. 28)

Mindfulness

Mindfulness is insight meditation applied to everyday life and involves bringing awareness to acts that we do each day. The rush and noise of our world make it difficult to be fully present. For example, we may try to relax by going for a walk, but we often take our problems with us on the walk. We may take with us a problem at work or our concern over how to pay the Visa bill, and we find at the end of our walk that we are so preoccupied that we haven't truly experienced the walk. We haven't really felt the air on our face, or looked at the trees, or felt the warmth of the sun. Nature can be very healing when we experience it directly, but our thoughts get in the way. In general, our preoccupations and thoughts can be a barrier to the world.

Another example of how it is difficult to be mindful is the way we often try to do several things at once. At home I can be watching television, reading the paper, and trying to carry on a conversation with my wife. In our attempts to fit everything in, our consciousness becomes fragmented. Our presence is diminished.

Another word for mindfulness is wholeheartedness, meaning that when we do something, we do it completely. Our consciousness is whole. Because mindfulness is so important to reconnecting ourselves with the world around us, I encourage my students to work on being mindful. There are many simple exercises that we can do to be more present. Mindfulness, then, can be seen as meditation in action.

We can start our practice by focusing on doing one thing at a time. The whole experience of preparing a meal, eating, and doing the dishes can be done mindfully. For example, as you cut the celery for the salad, just cut the celery. Don't try to solve the world's problems while you cut the celery. Sometimes we can be so preoccupied that we cut ourselves rather than the celery. Gradually, we find that by just cutting the celery, we can do a lot to heal ourselves and the world. Being fully present is a profoundly healing act. As we eat the meal, we can also focus our attention on the eating, chewing, and swallowing. Often we read the paper or watch television while we eat our meals, and as a result we taste very little. Finally, when doing the dishes, focus on the task. Feel the water as it cascades over your hands and the dishes. Often we can hardly wait to finish one task so that we can do something else. For example, as I do the dishes my mind will be on the hockey game that is about to start on television. As I watch the hockey game, my mind begins to drift to problems that I may face at work tomorrow. As we do one thing, our mind is on another. We seem to live in the future or the past.

One master of mindfulness is Thich Nhat Hanh, who has written several books on the subject. He suggests (1976) a variety of exercises in mindfulness:

Cleaning house

Divide your work into stages: straightening things and putting away books, scrubbing the toilet, scrubbing the bathroom, sweeping the floors and dusting. Allow a good length of time for each task. Move slowly, three times more slowly than usual. Fully focus your attention on each task. For example, while placing a book on the shelf, look at the book, be aware of what book it is, know that you are in the process of placing it on the shelf, intending to put it in that specific place. Know that your hand reaches for the book, and picks it up. Avoid any abrupt or harsh movement. Maintain mindfulness of the breath, especially when your thoughts wander.

A slow motion bath

Allow yourself 30 to 45 minutes to take a bath. Don't hurry for even one second. From the moment you prepare the bathwater to the moment you put on clean clothes, let every motion be light and slow. Be attentive of every movement. Place your attention to every part of your body, without discrimination or fear. Be mindful of each stream of water on your body. By the time you've finished, your mind should feel as peaceful and light as your body. Follow your breath. Think of yourself as being in a clean and fragrant lotus pond in the summer. (1976, pp. 86-87)

In a more recent book, Thich Nhat Hanh (1991) suggests a meditation for the telephone.

I recommend that the next time you hear the phone ring, just stay where you are, breathe in and out consciously, smile to yourself, and recite this verse: "Listen, listen. This wonderful sound brings me back to my true self." When the bell rings for the second time, you can repeat the verse, and your smile will be even more solid. When you smile, the muscles of your face relax, and your tension quickly vanishes. You can afford to practice breathing and smiling like this, because if the person calling has something important to say, she will certainly wait for at least three rings. When the phone rings for the third time, you can continue to practice breathing and smiling, as you walk to the phone slowly, with all your sovereignty. You are your own master. (p. 30)

I suggest that you start with very simple activities in developing mindfulness. Gradually you can bring your attention to more complex situations. Connected to insight sitting practice, mindfulness becomes a powerful way that we can carry our awareness into daily life. With mindfulness, meditation is not something that is fragmented or separated from the rest of life. Instead, our day becomes a seamless whole of awareness. We find that we live in the most empowering place, the eternal now.

Mantra

Mantra is simply using a word or phrase as a vehicle to awakening. It is repeated over and over in silent sitting meditation or as we do our daily activities. The word mantra "comes from the roots *man,* 'the mind,' and *tri,* 'to cross.' The mantram is that which enables us to cross the sea of the mind" (Easwaran, 1977, p. 43).

The mantra exists in almost all religions. As mentioned earlier, the Jesus prayer is a Christian mantra. *Hail Mary,* used in Catholicism, is another Christian mantra.

Gandhi repeated the mantra Ram throughout his life, and it was on his lips when he died. Other Hindu mantras using Ram include *Om Sri Ram jai Ram jai jai Ram.* This mantra simply means "May Joy prevail" (Easwaran, 1977, p. 58).

One of the most famous mantras in Buddhism is *Om mani padme hum,* which refers to the "jewel in the lotus of the heart" (Easwaran, 1977, p. 60). The lotus flower is used as a metaphor for purity of heart, which can be realized more fully by repeating this mantra.

In Judaism the phrase *Barukh attah Adonai* means "Blessed art thou, O Lord" (Easwaran, 1977, p. 60). By repeating this phrase, the devotee becomes more deeply connected to God.

In the Muslim faith the mantra *Bismillah ir-Rahman ir-Rahim* means "In the name of Allah, the merciful, the compassionate" (Easwaran, 1977, p. 61). According to Easwaran, "Orthodox Muslims say this mantra before they speak, as a reminder that everything we say and everything we do should be in accord with the will of God, in accord with the indivisible unity of life." (p. 61).

Once you have selected a mantra that seems to resonate with your being, stick with it. Do not shift mantras during meditation practice. It is also wise not to repeat your mantra to individuals who are not sympathetic to meditation practice. The mantra should not necessarily be a secret; it is just that you want to be able to approach meditation practice with a positive frame of mind.

Having chosen a mantra, you can begin practice. It is best to begin with your eyes open and to repeat the mantra out loud. Once you have a sense of the sound and the rhythm, you can begin to repeat it silently to yourself with your eyes closed. As you repeat the mantra, have the feeling that the mantra is autonomous; that is, it is repeating itself. You are not doing the mantra, but it is going on within you.

> That is all there is to meditating–just sitting peacefully, hearing the mantra in your mind, allowing it to change any way it wants–to get louder or softer–to disappear or return–to stretch out or speed up. . . . Meditation is like drifting on a stream in a boat without oars–because you need no oars–you are not going anywhere. (Carrington, 1977, p. 80)

It is also possible to repeat your mantra during the day. For example, the mantra can be repeated while riding the bus or subway. At work, if you begin to feel tense, you can work with the mantra to deal with the tension. The mantra can be used when you are walking, as the mantra can provide a silent rhythm to your walk. Other opportunities for mantra include times when you are sick or bored. Occasionally, we are presented with long stretches of time when there is nothing to do. Instead of turning on the television as relief from our boredom, we can practice mantra. Another good time for mantra is when you lie awake at night. Instead of letting random thoughts take over, which can often contribute to restlessness at night, try repeating a mantra. The silent rhythm will focus your mind and may help you return to sleep.

There are times when it is not appropriate to do mantra. For example, if you are doing any job or task that requires your full attention, such as driving or listening to music, the mantra will be an interference.

Eknath Easwaran (1977) has written a beautiful book on the mantra. He says:

> Once the mantram has become an integral part of our consciousness, all mantrams are the same. Whatever Holy Name we use, at this stage it is the perfect embodiment of the Lord of Love.
>
> The Holy Name reverberating in the depths of consciousness transfigures our entire vision of life. Just as the mantram transforms negative forces in consciousness into constructive power, so it now transforms all our perceptions of the everyday world into unbroken awareness of the unity of life. (pp. 246-247)

Visualization

Imagery can be a powerful source of inner growth. An image in our mind can have powerful effects. For example, if I am afraid of public speaking, just the image of seeing myself in front of an audience can make my heart beat faster. Guided imagery, or visualization, attempts to elicit images that can foster positive growth and awareness.

Visualization can bring about specific physiological changes. Studies have shown that when an individual imagines himself or herself running, small contractions take place in the muscles associated with running.

We also know that emotional changes can take place through visualization. For example, if we fear flying in an airplane, the image of this event can trigger fear and accompanying physiological changes. Similarly, a relaxing image, such as walking in a meadow, can lead to a lower heart rate, lower blood pressure, and relaxed muscles. Studies have been conducted in a number of areas, and Murphy (1992) claims that these "studies have shown that imagery practice can facilitate relief from various afflictions, among them depression, anxiety, insomnia, obesity, sexual problems, chronic pain, phobias, psychosomatic illnesses, cancer, and other diseases" (p. 372).

To work with visualization you should have, first of all, a quiet environment. Second, you need to be motivated; there must be some interest in what you are doing. Relaxed attention is also essential. You should be calm and focused on the task at hand. A general state of openness and receptivity is also important.

A simple visualization exercise to begin with is one in which you visualize an object, such as an orange.

Set an orange about two or three feet in front of you. Place the orange so that there are no other objects around it to distract your attention. . . . Relax and breathe deeply. . . . Now study the orange, notice its shape, color, any unusual markings, and so forth. . . . Now close your eyes. . . . See the image of the orange, for example, the shape, color, and any markings. . . . Now open your eyes and look at the orange. Compare it with the image you saw. Notice any differences. Now close your eyes and repeat the exercise.

Another simple and easy exercise is one in which you visualize a room from childhood. This requires recalling a more distant memory image than does the orange exercise.

Close your eyes. Imagine yourself in a room you associate with your childhood. Notice the furniture in the room. How is it arranged? Walk to the window and look out. What do you see? Now look around the room again. What colors do you notice? Are there any pictures on the wall? What does the rug look like? Are there any special objects in the room? Finally, notice the doors. Where do they lead?

Other visualizations can be used to help you gain insight into yourself and how you deal with various situations.

Close your eyes. . . . Relax deeply. . . . You are in a meadow and are feeling refreshed and invigorated. . . . You see a path in the meadow and begin to walk along it. You are enjoying yourself as you take in the scenery, the warmth of the sun, and the fresh air. . . . You know you are walking in the right direction. . . . As you continue on the walk, you can see an object ahead. . . . It is getting larger, and you can now see that it is a large stone wall. . . . As you draw closer to the wall, you see that it blocks the path and you cannot get around the wall or climb over it since it is so high. You now find yourself standing in front of the wall. What do you do?. . . . (Allow two minutes) . . . . Now slowly open your eyes and reflect on the visualization.

This guided fantasy can give you some insight into how you deal with formidable problems. The following guided imagery exercise can give you some insight into your future goals.

Close your eyes. . . . Relax. . . . You are in a meadow and you see a path. . . . You walk on the path. . . . Relax as you enjoy the surroundings. . . . You see birds in the air and hear them chirping. . . . The sky is blue and the air is fresh and clean. You begin to see that someone else is on the path and is gradually coming toward you. . . . You cannot see who the person is. . . . However, as the person gets closer you begin to see the resemblance to yourself. . . . You now see the person is you but 10 years older. . . . As you see yourself ten years from now, what do you look like?. . . . What clothes are you wearing?. . . . What does your face look like?. . . . What are your interests?. . . . What are you doing with yourself?. . . . What are your goals?. . . . Try to let an image appear of what you are becoming at that time. . . . Now slowly open your eyes. . . . Reflect on the visualization.

Some individuals find it difficult to see themselves or to imagine themselves in the future. If you have difficulty with this exercise, or with any other, you can come back to it at another time. You may find that images come easier the next time. The following guided imagery is more spiritually oriented:

Relax. Close your eyes. . . .You are in a meadow. . . .The sky is blue, and you see a hill in the distance. . . .What does the hill look like as you approach it?. . . . Is the hill large or small? . . . Is it rough and hard to climb or is its surface smooth and easy to scale? . . . You see a path going up the hill and you follow it. . . . Is the path wide or narrow? . . . What is the ground like around you as you begin to walk up the path? . . . Is there grass, or are there lots of rocks? . . . As you walk up this hill, notice the view. . . . Stop and look around. . . . How far can you see? . . . Now you begin to resume your walk. Smell the fresh air as you walk up the path. You feel invigorated and refreshed as you walk up the hill.

You begin to approach the top of the hill and there you see a temple. . . . As you approach the temple, what does it look like?. . . . Notice the form of the building as you approach it. As you approach the temple you feel peaceful and calm. . . . You walk to the door of the temple and take your shoes off. . . . There is an opening at the top of the temple roof, and sunlight is streaming through. . . . You walk to the light and stand under it and feel its radiance and warmth. . . . Let it permeate and rejuvenate your whole being. . . . You are now ready to go to the inner sanctuary. . . . There is a symbol or an image in the center of the room. . . . This symbol represents to you an educational ideal. Reflect on this symbol and its meaning for you . . . . (Allow a two or three minute pause). . . . Leave the temple and walk slowly down the hill. . . . Now you are reaching the bottom of the hill. Take the energy you have received from this journey and use it as you return to your daily life.

This guided imagery exercise contains a symbol that each person will imagine and interpret in his own way. Symbols are integral to the visualization process. Some common symbols found in fantasies and their possible meanings (as suggested in Samuels & Samuels) include:

Water: receptivity, passivity, calm
Ascent: growth, inward journey
Cross: tree of life, spiritual connectedness
Hill or Mountain: aims or ambitions
Light: creativity, unity, spiritual source
Sun: life force, healing spiritual wholeness
(Samuels & Samuels, 1975, p. 97)

A symbol can have many meanings, and we should not get too involved in interpreting them. However, if a symbol is persistent, you may want to work with it in meditation or other visualizations in order to see its meaning.

One of the best books on visualization is *Seeing with the Mind's Eye* (1975), by Samuels and Samuels. This book contains a number of visualizations that can be applied to being more creative, dealing with illness, or simply tapping our spiritual natures. The following exercise deals with spiritual development:

> You are now in a calm, relaxed state of being. To deepen this state you can imagine yourself traveling into space. Visualize yourself drifting weightlessly and effortlessly through space. See the deep blue-black color of space all around you. Watch stars and planets slowly recede as you move past them further and further into space. As you see each star recede, you will become more and more relaxed, in a deeper and deeper state of mind. Now visualize an area of diffuse white light ahead of you. Picture yourself moving closer and closer to this area of light until you are bathed by its luminosity and can feel its energy. Travel into the light, toward its center. Visualize the center of the light as a space beyond light and darkness. In this space, you will feel open and clear. You will begin to see images before you. Look at them as long as they appear. These are pure images. They have a life of their own, and they will appear and extinguish of their own accord. If any of the images evoke disturbing feelings in you, do not be afraid. Simply allow the images to pass.
>
> Stay in this space as long as you wish. You can receive pure images whenever you go to it. To return to your everyday state of mind simply visualize yourself moving back through space to the place where you started. Count from 1 to 3. Then open your eyes. (Samuels & Samuels, 1975, p. 156)

If we feel a connection to a particular spiritual teacher, we can visualize the presence of that person and can imagine the energy, love, and compassion flowing from that person into our own hearts. Visualizing the presence of another person is called kything. Savary and Berne (1988) define kything as a conscious act of spiritual presence. One example of kything they cite is from Viktor Frankl's book *Man's Search for Meaning*. One of the ways that Frankl survived in the concentration camp was to imagine the presence of his wife.

> As my friend and I stumbled on for miles, slipping on icy spots, supporting each other time and time again, dragging one another up and onward, nothing was said but we both knew; each of us was thinking of his wife. Occasionally I looked at the sky, where the stars were fading and the pink light of the morning was beginning to spread behind a dark bank of clouds. But my mind clung to my wife's image, imagining it with an uncanny acuteness. I heard her answering me, saw her smile, her frank and encouraging look. Real or not, her look was then more luminous than the sun which was beginning to rise. (Cited in Savary and Berne, 1988, p. 68)

Savary and Berne (1988) talk about three modes of presence: physical, psychological, and spiritual. Kything is at the spiritual level and can be described simply as a form of communion.

Movement Meditation

In movement meditation, we bring a heightened awareness to bodily movement. One approach to movement meditation is hatha yoga, and in this section I would like to outline some basic asanas, or postures, from hatha yoga. Hatha yoga, I believe, complements sitting meditation because it keeps the body loose and flexible. Even if someone is doing walking or running, it is also recommended that they do stretching exercises as in hatha yoga. Hatha yoga has played an important role in my own life. In 1969, like many young American males, I faced the possibility of being sent to Vietnam. After much inner turmoil, I decided that I could not participate in the war if I was called. This decision, and the uncertainty of my draft status, put me under a great deal of stress. I was having trouble coping and doing my work as a university instructor. As a result, I began to search for some integrative mechanism to deal with my inner and outer concerns. In my search, I read about the positive benefits of yoga and thus began to practice the asanas. After about six weeks I began to notice changes in myself. I was generally calmer and more relaxed in situations that only a few weeks before had been terrifying. In general, I found that I was better able to deal with the trauma of the draft. I gradually became more interested in the philosophy behind yoga, as I was interested in the background of a method that had such a positive impact on my life. This was the beginning of my interest in transpersonal issues and methods.

In the following section I outline some asanas that are basic to the practice of yoga. It should be noted that an individual can approach hatha yoga as a method to attain specific benefits or as part of an overall path of spiritual practice. In the first instance, the focus will be on practicing the asanas. In the latter case, the asanas are seen in relation to meditation and other spiritual practices. Within this framework, the individual often does asanas because they facilitate meditative practice. Hatha yoga can let the individual witness the relationship between body and mind as well as facilitate overall integration.

Whatever your perspective, you should start slowly. Do not push yourself too far with the asanas or try the advanced postures before you feel you are ready. Allow approximately 20 to 30 minutes for your practice, and do the asanas gently. Do not overdo it. Also, relax between postures, as this allows the effects of the asana to sink in. It is better to do a few asanas well than to rush through several exercises. As you proceed through the asanas, listen to your body. If any movement is at all painful, take it easy. Work slowly with the asana so that you can listen to what your body is saying.

It is best to do the asanas either before a meal or at least two hours after you have eaten. Early morning and evening are probably the best times to practice the asanas. In the morning you will find that you are somewhat stiffer than later in the day, but the asanas help you get going in the morning without several cups of coffee. In the evening asanas will help you relax and ease daily tensions. If you are combining meditation and asanas, it is helpful to do the asanas before meditation.

The following asanas are given in the order in which they should be performed. The order allows the body and spine to be worked in various directions and for each asana to complement the previous posture.

Cobra

Lie on your stomach with palms down on the floor. Relax. The hands should be at shoulder level. Now raise your head, slowly, as far as you can and then push with your hands, keeping the lower half of the body on the floor. Breathe in as you arch backwards Hold the position for about 15 seconds. Slowly come back down and exhale.

For maximum benefit, repeat the exercise. This asana loosens the spine and improves the posture.

Cobra

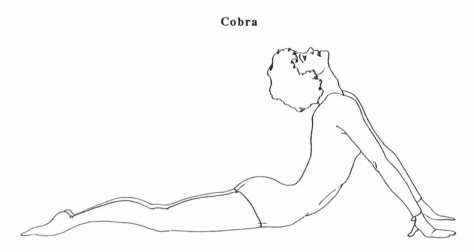

Locust

The locust follows the cobra and helps loosen the lower part of the spine. It also brings blood to the brain and relieves tension in the lower back.

You can begin with the half locust. Lie face down with hands along the sides and palms facing up. Now breathe in and raise the right foot and leg, keeping the knee straight. Stretch the leg and hold for 8 to 10 seconds. Slowly lower the leg, as you exhale. Now repeat this movement with the left leg. You should do the half locust before attempting the full locust.

Half   Locust

In the full locust the hands are clinched into fists and slid under the thighs. Inhale, raising both legs. Keep the knees straight. Hold for approximately 15 seconds and breathe normally. Slowly lower the legs and exhale. Relax.

Full   Locust

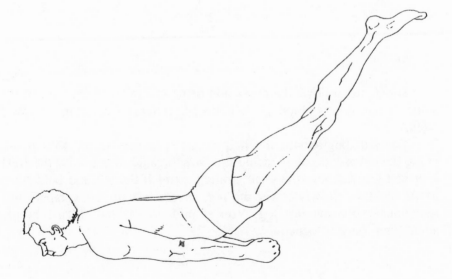

The Bow

This asana completes the arching of the spine in the backward position. It stretches the spine and also helps massage the abdominal organs.

Lie on the stomach and reach back with the hands to grasp the ankles. Breathe in and slowly raise your head and knees and make a bow. Hold for about 15 seconds and breathe normally. Now come down slowly and exhale. Repeat once. Do not spread the ankles but keep them together as you do this exercise.

Bow 1

Bow 2

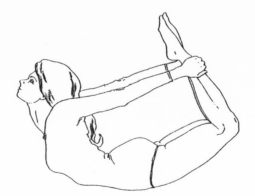

Head-Knee Pose

This is a forward-stretching exercise that helps you relax the muscles of the body and tone the liver, kidneys, and digestive tract.

Begin by sitting erect with legs straight in front. Now, draw in your right foot with your hands and tuck it in to the pelvic area. Inhale and slowly raise your arms above your head and bend toward the knees. Exhale and stretch as far as you can without forcing it. Once you have reached your limit, hold for 15 seconds. Inhale as you come up.

Head-Knee Pose

Back Stretch

Begin this exercise lying with your back on the floor. Slowly raise your arms and back off the floor. Move the back into an upright position and put your hands on your thighs. Continue moving, stretching forward as far as you can, without overdoing it. Breathe out as you stretch forward, and breathe normally as you hold the stretch position for about 20 seconds. Repeat.

As you practice this exercise, you may notice that you are able to bend slightly farther each time.

Back   Stretch

The Shoulder Stand

In the shoulder stand we put the body in a position that essentially reverses the effects of gravity on the body. By reversing the flow of blood to the head and putting the organs of the body in a different position, the asana is a stimulus to the brain as well as a relaxant to the body.

Begin by lying flat, with your back on the floor and your hands on the ground. Exhale and slowly raise your legs to an upright position. As they move up, put your hands on the middle of your back. Now extend your legs upright. Keep your legs straight. It is helpful to have someone check your position so that you do not become lopsided. Hold this for about three minutes and gradually increase to four or five minutes. You do not need to point the toes; instead, let the legs become relaxed.

This exercise can also be practiced during the day to help revitalize the body.

Shoulder Stand 1

Shoulder Stand 2

The Plow

This asana is best practiced after the shoulder stand. The plow helps stretch the entire body and stimulates the thyroid gland and the spine. This exercise should be done very slowly.

Begin by lying on your back with the palms face down on the floor. Slowly bring the legs up and lower them over the head. Keep the knees straight and make sure that you lower the legs slowly. If you rush this exercise, you can strain the neck. It may take some time before you can lower the legs until the feet touch the ground. If your feet do not touch the ground, leave them dangling in the air with the knees straight.

While you are moving, you should keep your concentration on the place where there is movement. When you are in the fully stretched position, the point of concentration can be on the thyroid gland.

The Plow

Fish Pose

This pose provides a good counter position to the two previous poses, since it stretches the thyroid area and spine in the opposite direction, thus bringing the body back into balance. It also assists deep breathing and massages organs in the abdominal area.

Fish Pose

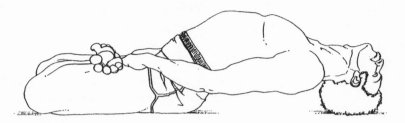

Begin the position lying on your back, hands at the side with the elbows on the ground. Lean back on the elbows and arch the back. Now move the head back and attempt to move the head so that the top of the head is on the floor and you are looking along the floor upside down. As you reach this position, remove the elbows from the ground and place your hands on your thighs. Your weight is now on the head and the buttocks area. Hold for approximately one-third the time you spent in the shoulder stand. The fish can also be performed from a kneeling position or with the legs crossed.

Half Twist

This asana twists the spine in a different direction than the previous exercises. The half twist completes the cycle of spine movements that you have been doing during this particular series of asanas.

The complete half twist can be approached through a series of movements. To begin, sit on the floor with your legs straight out front. Then twist your body to the right and place your hands on the ground at your right. Do this also to the left side.

Now return to your original position and grasp your right leg and place it over your left leg. The right foot should be beside the left leg. Twist your body to the right and place the hands on the ground. If you cannot place your hands on the ground, slide your left arm over your raised knee and grasp the other knee. Now place your other arm on the ground behind you and turn your head to the right.

Half   Twist

To do the full half twist, sit with your legs straight ahead. Pull in the left foot and place it in the pelvic area. Now lift your right leg over the left so that the right foot is as far back as possible, and still on the ground. Next twist your body to the right and slide the left elbow over the knee. Now grab the left knee with the left hand. Put your right hand as far around behind you as possible and turn your head to the right. Hold for 15 seconds and then slowly unwind. Repeat with the opposite side.

Half Lotus Position

The lotus position is difficult for most people to achieve. It is better to attempt the half lotus or simply cross your legs in a comfortable position.

Half Lotus

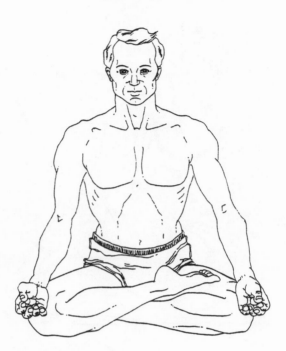

Many of the asanas just described will help in sitting in a half lotus or simple cross-legged position. If you use any of these positions for meditation, then hatha yoga exercises will help you in your meditation.

Lovingkindness

This meditation can either be done as a meditation in itself or combined with other meditations described earlier. For example, it can done at the beginning or end of a meditation period. Like mantra, it can also be done during the day while you are standing in line, riding the bus, or some doing some other activity that does not demand your total attention. The essence of this meditation is first to center ourselves in the heart area and to contact a basic warmth there. After connecting with the heart we then attempt to share this warmth and energy with others. For example, one could use the following approach:

> May I be well, happy, and peaceful.
> May my family be well, happy, and peaceful.
> May my friends be well, happy, and peaceful.
> May my neighbors be well, happy, and peaceful.
> May my colleagues be well, happy, and peaceful.
> May all people that I meet be well, happy, and peaceful.
> May all people who may have injured me by deed, speech, or thought be well, happy, and peaceful.
> May all beings on this planet be well, happy, and peaceful.
> May all beings in this universe be well, happy, and peaceful.

This approach starts with those who are emotionally closest to us and then moves out. Another approach is move out geographically.

> May I be well, happy, and peaceful.
> May all beings in this room be well, happy, and peaceful.
> May all beings in this building be well, happy, and peaceful.
> May all beings in this neighborhood be well, happy, and peaceful.
> May all beings in this town or city be well, happy, and peaceful.
> May all beings in this district or county be well, happy, and peaceful.
> May all beings in this state or province be well, happy, and peaceful.
> May all beings in this country be well, happy, and peaceful.
> May all beings in this hemisphere be well, happy, and peaceful.
> May all beings on this planet be well, happy, and peaceful.
> May all beings in this universe be well, happy, and peaceful.

When you are doing the lovingkindness meditation it is possible to visualize the people to whom you are sending these thoughts. I start my classes with this exercise, and I find that it has added immeasurably to the tone and feel of the class. Many of my students have commented on it as well. A friend of mine, Diana Hughes, who is director of the Rudolf Steiner Centre in Toronto, states that holistic education is the invisible space between teacher and student. I have found that the lovingkindness exercise does much to augment this space.

GETTING STARTED

If you have never meditated before, you may want to try the different methods for a while until you find the one you are most comfortable with. Again, the approach will be probably be congruent with your orientation—intellectual, emotional, emphasizing action, or physical. Once you have settled on an approach, stick with it. If you keep changing, your practice will never deepen.

To begin meditation practice, sit comfortably with your head, neck, and chest in a straight line. You can sit in a chair or cross-legged on a cushion or bench. Most important, you should be in a position where you won't be shifting around a lot during the meditation. It is probably best to meditate at least one hour after eating. The times that seem to be most popular for meditation are early in the morning upon arising, before dinner, or late in the evening. You should choose a place free of distractions. If you have a room for meditation, fine; if not, then a corner of a bedroom can also be arranged so that it is conducive to meditation. Once you have settled on a time and place, others in the household should be made aware that you are not to be disturbed unless there is something urgent. However, you should not be unreasonable about your practice. For example, if there are young children in the household, you should probably not choose to meditate right before dinner, as this usually is a busy time around the household and meditation practice could interfere with the needs of the family. Meditation should be done so that family life patterns are not drastically disturbed.

A period of 20 minutes of meditation is appropriate for beginning the practice. As you commit yourself to a particular method, then you can lengthen the period to 30 or 40 minutes. During meditation you can look at your watch to check the time. Timers are also available, but it is perfectly fine to check a watch or clock during the meditation period. At the end, remain seated for a minute or two, thus allowing a space between the meditation and the resumption of daily activities.

REFERENCES

Carrington, Patricia. (1977). *Freedom in meditation*. New York: Doubleday.

Easwaran, Eknath. (1977). *The mantram handbook: Formulas for transformation*. Berkeley, CA: Nilgri Press.

French, B. M. (Trans.) (1974). *The way of a pilgrim*. New York: Ballantine.

Goldstein, Joseph. (1976). *The experience of insight: A natural unfolding*. Santa Cruz, CA: Unity Press.

Hanh, T. N. (1976). *The miracle of mindfulness! A manual on meditation*. Boston: Beacon Press.

——. (1991). *Peace is every step: The path of mindfulness in everyday life*. New York: Bantam.

Kabat-Zinn, Jon. (1990). *Full catastrophe living: Using the wisdom of your body and mind to face stress, pain and illness*. New York: Delacorte Press.

Krishnamurti, J. (1963). *Life ahead*. Wheaton, IL: Theosophical Publishing House.

LeShan, Lawrence. (1974). *How to meditate*. Boston: Little, Brown, and Company.

Murphy, Michael. (1992). *The future of the body: Explorations into the further evolution of human nature*. New York: Jeremy Tarcher.

Ornish, Dean. (1990). *Dr. Dean Ornish's program for recovering from heart disease*. New York: Random House.

Samuels, M., & Samuels, N. (1975). *Seeing with the mind's eye*. New York: Random House.

Savary, L. M., & Berne, p. H. (1988). *Kything: The art of spiritual presence*. Mahwah, NJ: Paulist Press.

Smith, H. (1986). *The religions of man*. New York: Harper Perennial.

Williams, Redford. (1989). *The trusting heart: Great news about type A behavior*. New York: Times.

5

Contemplatives and Their Practices

Perhaps the most powerful examples of contemplative practice come from individuals who made contemplation central to their spiritual lives. The lives and practices of these persons can inspire our own practice. The descriptions of contemplatives is necessarily brief here, as the aim is to describe individuals from a variety of traditions and their basic approaches to contemplative practices. Five individuals are discussed–Buddha, Teresa of Avila, Emerson, Gandhi, and Merton.

BUDDHA

Although Buddha was born almost 2,500 years ago, his teachings seem to be particularly relevant today. Buddha asked that we simply observe our own experience in a wakeful manner. The Buddha's emphasis on watching our own personal experience as a spiritual practice seems particularly appropriate to our age. We have become suspicious of dogmas and rituals. In contrast, the Buddha avoided dogmatic assertion and encouraged each individual to be the agent of his or her own awakening through mindfulness and meditation.

Buddha, whose name was Siddhartha Gautama, was born in the sixth century B.C. in India. He was the son of a wealthy aristocrat who lived in what is today southern Nepal. His family was part of the aristocratic military class, which was equal in status to the priestly Brahmin class. Thus, Siddhartha grew up in very affluent surroundings. His father doted on the boy and made sure that all of his needs were met;

he also wanted his son protected from suffering and distress. Siddhartha's father forbade his son from leaving the palace grounds, because he did not want him to witness disease or death.

One of the main stories associated with the Buddha's youth is that he grew curious about what was outside the palace and one day left with his charioteer, Channa. When traveling around the city, he first saw an old man. He then saw a very sick person, and finally he saw a corpse.

Siddhartha began to reflect on how anyone could truly be happy if there was aging, sickness, and death. He asked people in the palace, but no one provided an adequate explanation. One day, outside the palace, he ran into a wandering holy man whose simple and calm presence suggested to him that what he needed to know was beyond the gates of the palace. He resolved to leave the palace in search of spiritual wisdom, even though he was now married and had a young son. One night he left the palace with Channa. Although on the surface leaving one's family appears cruel, most spiritual traditions indicate that ultimately we may have to put our spiritual quest above all other matters. For example, Christ indicated that his teachings could divide families. There is also a tradition in India suggesting that at some point in life (usually around age 40 or 50), it is acceptable to leave the family and devote oneself to the spiritual life.

The Buddha's first teacher was Alara Kalama. Kalama was a hermit, but Kalama's teachings, although they were helpful, did not satisfy Siddhartha's deepest concerns. Siddhartha then entered a long period of extreme asceticism. For about six years he fasted and meditated with five other seekers. Although Siddhartha learned to concentrate his mind during this period, he was not able to come to any understanding about age, sickness, and death. The fasting had also weakened him considerably. Siddhartha came then to the understanding that the body should not be abused in the search for spiritual understanding. He began taking food to restore his body. His five fellow seekers believed that the Buddha had given up the right way to enlightenment, so they left him.

Siddhartha, after nourishing himself, now began his famous meditation under the Bodhi tree, which was located in what today is the town of Bodhgaya in India. Siddhartha was around 30 years of age. When he began his meditation, a young woman named Sujata brought him a golden bowl of rice milk. According to one story, Siddhartha drank from the bowl and then placed it in a stream, where it proceeded to float upstream against the current. The bowl came to rest in front of the place where the Serpent King lived. This story metaphorically represents Buddhism's relation to nature, since the Serpent King signifies the wisdom of nature. Other stories concerning the Buddha's life also show the connection between his teachings and the natural world. As we struggle to overcome the environmental degradation of this age, such stories take on added significance.

In the second chapter, I cited Campbell's description of how the Buddha was tempted by the God Mara. At one point the Buddha simply pointed to the ground, signifying how his enlightenment was grounded in the earth itself. Buddha's enlightenment is the great event in Buddhism; at this time he gained understandings that were later expressed in the four noble truths and the eightfold path.

The Buddha maintained that each of us can attain enlightenment through meditative practice. Enlightenment is not something that is separate or remote; rather, it is available to us in the here and now. Central to this experience of enlightenment is witnessing the interdependence of all matter and energy. The Buddha saw very clearly how all things arise and then pass away in a deep and connected way.

After this experience, the Buddha decided that he must share his understanding with others on earth. The Buddha had attained nirvana and could have remained detached from human striving, but instead, out of infinite compassion for all beings, he taught and shared his discoveries with others. The decision to teach and serve even though one has attained enlightenment is at the center of the bodhisatva tradition in Buddhism. The bodhisatva defers his or her own nirvana till all beings have attained liberation. Central to Buddhism, then, is compassion. Compassion arises from understanding at the deepest level that all is connected and that separation from others is an illusion.

The Buddha began his teaching by returning to his former companions. They were struck by the Buddha's radiance and were drawn to him immediately, and he began teaching them. He shared the four noble truths, which include:

1. Suffering is inherent in existence.
2. Suffering and dissatisfaction arise from our grasping and our sense of separateness (created by the ego).
3. We can let go of our grasping and sense of separation.
4. The release from ego and greed can occur through the eightfold path.

The eightfold path involves:

1. Right understanding.
2. Right purpose.
3. Right speech.
4. Right conduct.
5. Right livelihood.
6. Right effort.
7. Right awareness.
8. Right concentration, or meditation.

Right understanding refers to witnessing the four noble truths. *Right purpose* involves a sense that we are on a path and are committed to spiritual practice. *Right speech* and conduct mean that we do not intentionally harm others by speech or action. *Right livelihood* suggests that our work should not involve any activity that would harm others or contribute to their suffering. *Right effort* refers to the fact that each of us must make an individual effort to awaken. *Right awareness* means that in our daily actions we are mindful or fully present. Finally, we need to *contemplate and concentrate* the mind through meditative practice.

Through his teachings and presence, the Buddha inspired his followers to become monks and to go out into the world to teach. The monks approached teaching not as proselytizing but simply as setting the example of their own practice. The Buddha also encouraged his followers not to engage in intellectual or theoretical debates. He felt that intellectual exchanges sidetrack us from our path to wisdom and compassion. In his book *Buddhist Teaching of Totality*, Garma C. C. Chang wrote:

> Buddha was never [merely] a philosopher; His primary concern was to point out the way to liberation—liberation from the deep-rooted attachment to a delusory self which is the source of all passion-desires and their resultant pains and frustrations. Philosophical speculations were persistently rejected and denounced by Buddha as useless, foolish and unsalutary. Actually, in Buddha's teaching we do not find a philosophy; what we find is a significant therapeutic device, the instruction on how to get rid of the deep ego-clinging attitude. (Cited in Ross, 1980, p. 28)

Central to Buddhism is the connection between thought and action. Through meditation and mindfulness, we begin to root out inconsistencies between thought and action. By seeing connections at all levels, we begin to live more in harmony with the basic teachings, and they become living reality. The following Buddhist saying captures this idea very well:

> The thought manifests as the word,
> The word manifests as the deed,
> The deed develops into habit,
> And the habit hardens into character.
> So watch the thought
> And its way with care,
> And let it spring from love
> Born out of respect for all beings. (source unknown)

The simple attention of witnessing how our thoughts give rise to certain actions can free us and make us more compassionate. This process of meditation and mindfully watching our thoughts and actions is an organic one. We are not imposing a set of beliefs on ourselves or others; we are simply trying to *see,* or to be fully awake. This process leads to a gradual unfolding or flowering of what Buddhists call the dharma, the truth or law underlying all things.

The Buddha taught for almost 50 years. In that time he taught all manner of people and accepted women into the order of monks. He did return to his home so he could share his teachings with his father, wife, and son.

The Buddha died when he was about 80 years old. The Buddha still taught as he neared his death. He told his disciples, "Work with diligence. Be lamps unto yourselves. Betake yourselves to no external refuge. Look not for refuge to anyone beside yourself. Hold fast to the Truth as to a lamp" (cited in Ross, 1980, p. 36).

SAINT TERESA OF AVILA

Teresa of Avila lived in sixteenth-century Spain and is one the most revered of all contemplatives. Although Teresa was Catholic, her father came from Jewish ancestry. He married twice, as his first wife died after having two children; his second wife had eight children, including seven boys who all became conquistadors during the time when Spain encouraged exploration of the globe. Teresa's mother died after giving birth to eight children, and since Teresa was the oldest she helped with raising the boys. However, around age 20 she decided to join a convent. She chose the Incarnation order, which was more relaxed than many other orders.

The Incarnation convent in Avila was crowded, with about two hundred women living within its walls, and was open to visitors who might bring food or gifts to the nuns. These visitors included men who were sometimes interested in innocent flirtation with the nuns. By all accounts, Teresa was beautiful, and the men who came to the convent were immediately attracted to her. Eventually, she found the male company such a distraction to her vocation that she became sick. Thus she went back to her home to recover. While at home she read *The Third Spiritual Alphabet*, by Francisco de Osuna. This book introduced Teresa to contemplative prayer and provided the initial impetus to her contemplative practice. Teresa was sick for almost two years. At one point she was so weak and ill that she almost died.

Teresa returned to the convent and found that she was subject to the same temptations. She still found herself holding court in the parlor at the convent. There were many male visitors, and apparently one, who has remained nameless, attracted her attention and affections. Teresa struggled with her conflicts for many years, until she was 40. At that time she experienced a second spiritual rebirth, the first being her first sickness and recovery when she was in her early twenties. Carol Lee Flinders (1993) describes the event:

> One minute Teresa was walking past an image of the crucified Christ recently placed in a corridor of the Incarnation, and the next, they tell us, she was on her knees, sobbing, repenting of nearly twenty years' indifference, and begging God to strengthen her once and for all. In truth, this sudden conversion had been a long time in the making. (p. 169)

Flinders explains that this conversion was the result of years of contemplative prayer in which Teresa would begin the time of prayer feeling conflicted, but at the end would say in her own words that she felt a "greater quiet and delight."

At this same time someone gave her a copy of St. Augustine's *Confessions*, and she wept when she read it. Teresa found Augustine's spiritual path similar to her own. His narrative inspired her contemplation, much as the *Spiritual Alphabet* had done twenty years earlier.

The parlor was no longer a threat to her spiritual life as she found that her contemplation deepened and that she could communicate with God as an intimate friend. She said: "No longer do I want you to converse with men, but with angels" (1946, Vol. 1, p. 155).

Through contemplation Teresa seemed to find a deeper spiritual voice. Teresa traveled from the convent in Avila to found seventeen Carmelite convents and four monasteries. She traveled all over Spain in a donkey cart. The efforts in each community to establish a convent were not always well received, but Teresa's powerful presence helped forge the establishment of each convent. Once established, the convents were often fraught with conflicts between the nuns, and she had to resolve the problems through letters or a personal visit. All these problems contributed to her declining health; arthritis, heart disease, malaria, and a broken shoulder that was never properly set and gave her constant pain were among her illnesses. Despite these difficulties, her literary output was tremendous during this whole period. She was ordered to write her *Autobiography* to make the nature of her contemplative prayer clear to others. This was the period of the Inquisition in Spain, and her ecstatic contemplative states were well known. The Dominicans who ran the Inquisition were suspicious of silent prayer.

Her contemporaries claimed that her writing was much like her speech. Although it tended to wander, it was invariably direct and accessible; in short, she developed her own voice. She did not try to emulate the learned style of the Dominicans but instead adopted a vernacular that disarmed her opposition (Flinders, 1993, p. 176). Her writing was filled with direct images. She referred to one hermit saint as someone who was made of "nothing but tree roots" She wrote of the difficulties in meditation in a way that is understandable to any meditator no matter what tradition he or she comes from, saying, "This intellect is so wild that it doesn't seem be anything else than a frantic madman no one can tie down" (cited in Flinders, 1993, p. 177).

In the *Autobiography* she describes the stages of mental prayer as the "four waters," and each of these stages refers to how one waters a garden. The first water is drawn from the well. The main challenge at this beginning stage is distractedness, and the essential aspect of contemplative practice is simply determination.

The second stage refers to a system of aqueducts and a waterwheel whose crank must be turned. Less effort is now required than in the first stage, as one begins to experience grace, which allows one to be "nearer the light."

The third stage is characterized by a river or spring. Our task here is to direct the flow of the river, and this becomes more effortless as we align ourselves with God. We experience more joy and delight at this stage.

The final stage is where we experience union with God. The metaphor that Teresa uses here is one of rainfall: "This rain comes from Heaven to fill and saturate the whole of this garden " (1946, Vol. 1, p. 108). This union, however, is not an ethereal one divorced from our humanity. She says, "It is an important thing that while we are living and are human we have human support." She also felt the body should not be denied or abused.

Her writing was much like the water she describes; it simply flowed. She wrote, "I realize clearly that it is not I who am saying this; for I am not putting it together with my own understanding and afterwards I cannot tell how I have managed to say it all" (1946, Vol. 1, p. 86).

Her next book was *The Way of Perfection*, which also describes the contemplative life. Before one approaches contemplative practice, she suggests, there must be love, detachment, and humility. For Teresa love is best seen as spiritual friendship, where we share a concern for the other person's spiritual growth.

Detachment means that we are not overly involved with others or the petty things in life. Seeing things from a larger perspective, we develop "freedom of spirit" (cited in Flinders, 1993, p. 183).

Finally, humility involves not making excuses for oneself. She refers particularly to her own life and how her friend, St. John of the Cross, told her one day, "You have a fine way of excusing yourself" (cited in Flinders, p. 183). Teresa stressed the qualities of love, detachment, and humility because the environment that one practices contemplation in is as important as the prayer itself. If one lives in a place where these qualities do not exist, then contemplation becomes much more difficult to practice.

In *The Way of Perfection*, Teresa argues for the value of silent prayer. She suggests that within each person is an "extremely rich palace, built entirely of gold and precious stones" (cited in Flinders, 1993, p. 184). It is difficult to access this palace, and she makes particular reference to women.

> For, as we women are not learned, or *fine-witted*, we
> need all things to help us realize that we actually have
> something within us incomparably more precious than
> anything we see outside. (1946, Vol. 2, p. 117)

She often addresses women in her work, and she never wavers in her
assumption that contemplative prayer is the "birthright of women as
well as men" (Flinders, p. 184).

Her third major book, *Interior Castle,* was written when she was
age 62. She starts this book with the following lines: "I began to think
of the soul as if it were a castle made out of a single diamond or of
very clear crystal, in which there are many rooms" (1946, Vol 2, p.
201). In this book she describes seven stages of contemplation. The
first three stages have to do with settling down, while the fourth stage is
a transition period from the natural to the supernatural. The fifth stage
is where one finds union and is born into a new life with Christ. Here
Teresa uses the metaphor of a silkworm, describing how the soul dies
in the cocoon and is transformed into a white butterfly. The sixth stage
can be a long period where the person experiences further trials to
prepare her for the final stage. The final stage she finds difficult to
describe; she says she may not have fully realized this dimension of
spiritual life. Nevertheless, she describes the last stage as a life with
Christ where we experience limitless love.

Teresa's struggles were many as she traveled across Spain setting
up new convents. Flinders (1993) compares her approach to her work
to Gandhi's:

> On paper her task sounds simple enough: to reform a
> contemplative order. Over and over, though, what
> should have been simple turned into a nightmare of
> rancorous contention. I have drawn comparisons
> between Catherine of Siena and Gandhi, but perhaps he
> and Teresa are even closer in spirit. Dazzled by
> Gandhi's mastery of nonviolence as a tool for political
> reform—the acts of civil disobedience and the extended
> fasts—most commentators overlook his knack for com-
> promise. Without caving in on essentials, he knew how
> to draw opponents over by giving way in small things.
> He knew how to find the few areas where conflicting
> interests happened to overlap and then to enlarge them
> little by painstaking little. He was never abstract, always

personal. Teresa operated in much the same way, drawing to her cause and into her affections individuals who did not always seem worthy of that honor. She did so for the same reason Gandhi would: the work at hand was far too urgent to be postponed until perfect men and women came along to undertake it. (p. 89)

Teresa of Avila is another example of someone who combined contemplation and action in powerful ways. She shows that the contemplative life is a powerful source for acting creatively in the world.

EMERSON

Ralph Waldo Emerson is widely studied and quoted today. John Dewey called Emerson the "Philosopher of Democracy" and "the one citizen of the New World fit to have his name uttered in the same breath with that of Plato" (cited in Allen, 1981, p. 645).

Emerson's appeal lies, in part, in the fact that he called on the individual to trust his or her own powers, particularly the intuitive sense, as a basis for action. He referred to this intuitive sense as moral sentiment, and he urged individuals to be in touch with their own inwardness as a source of moral action.

Another reason for the interest lies simply with the man himself. Oliver Wendell Holmes (1885, 1980), a contemporary of Emerson and a critic of his mysticism, nevertheless said the following in his book *Ralph Waldo Emerson*:

> Judged by his life, Emerson comes very near our best ideal of humanity. No matter of what he wrote or spoke, his words, his tones, his looks, carried the evidence of a sincerity which pervaded them all and was to his eloquence and poetry like the water of crystallization; without which they would effloresce into mere rhetoric.
>
> There are living organisms so transparent that we can see their hearts beating and their blood flowing through their glassy tissues. So transparent was the life of Emerson; so clearly did the true nature of the man show through it. What he taught others to be, he was himself. His deep and sweet humanity won him love and

> reverence everywhere among those whose natures were
> capable of responding to the highest manifestations of
> character. (pp. 324-325)

In short, Emerson's thinking, writing, and life were integrated. It is this integration of his work and thought that is so appealing. It is not just his writing that strikes a responsive chord today, but the authenticity of the man himself.

Emerson was born on May 25, 1803, in Boston, Massachusetts. His father, a minister, died when Emerson was eight. His mother managed to support the family so that Emerson and his brothers could go to school. Emerson studied at Harvard, and he too became a minister. He married shortly after beginning his Unitarian ministry, but his first wife died of tuberculosis less than 18 months later. Emerson was to suffer many personal tragedies in his life, including the death of a son; however, these events did not alter his optimistic philosophy or his humane disposition.

After the death of his first wife, Emerson examined his religious beliefs and resigned from his ministerial post in Boston. He felt that the rituals of organized religion tended to ossify the individual's direct contact with God. Thus, he began the career as lecturer and writer that was to continue for the rest of his life. In both the United States and England, he was known as the foremost lecturer of the nineteenth century. John Trowbridge (1903) said, "Emerson was no orator. . . . He had no gift of extemporary utterance, no outburst of improvisation. But in the expression of ethical thought, or in downright moral vehemence, I believed and still believe him unequaled" (cited in McAleer, 1989, p. 308). James Russell Lowell agreed: "I have heard some great speakers and some accomplished orators, but never any that so moved and persuaded me as he" (cited in McAleer, 1989, p. 493).

Moncure Conway has said that Emerson's address at Harvard Divinity School in 1838 "stands in the moral history of America where the Declaration of Independence stands in its political history." (Cited in McAleer, p. 248-9). John McAleer (1984) summarizes this address by Emerson:

> In strictly theological terms, the basic message of the
> Divinity address was that man by responding intuitively,
> through Nature, to the moral sentiment expresses his
> divinity. Christ taught that "God incarnates himself in
> man." Christian leaders have failed their fellowman

> because they have neglected to explore "the Moral
> Nature . . . as the fountain of the established teaching in
> society." They have fossilized Christianity by putting
> too much emphasis on formal ritual. True faith is
> attained only when a man experiences a personal aware-
> ness of the Supreme Spirit dwelling within him. (p. 249)

This address caused a storm of controversy, and Emerson was not invited back to Harvard for thirty years.

Although Emerson did not like the term transcendentalist, he was considered part of the group identified by that name. Transcendentalists argued that individuals are most capable of moral behavior when they are in touch with their own conscience or that "still small voice within." The transcendentalists included Margaret Fuller, Walt Whitman, Bronson Alcott, and Henry David Thoreau. Emerson was mentor to these individuals, particularly to Thoreau, who also lived in Concord. Emerson encouraged Thoreau in his Walden venture.

Although Emerson was not a social activist, he was willing to take a stand regarding critical social issues. He spoke out against slavery and opposed the expulsion of the Cherokee Indians from Georgia. He was also supportive of women's rights. Although he was capable of deep moral indignation, he abhorred fanaticism and always held a deep compassion for his opponent.

Emerson lived most of his life in Concord, Massachusetts, with his second wife, Lidian. Emerson was deeply loved by those who knew him. Late in his life, his house burned, and the citizens of Concord had his home rebuilt while Emerson traveled. He died in 1882.

Emerson was not a rigorous philosopher who developed a comprehensive philosophical system. In fact, he coined the phrase "consistency is the hobgoblin of little minds." He was an eclectic, and he drew on many sources. In particular, he was influenced by Plato, Neoplatonists such as Plotinus, and Goethe. He sensed the inadequacy of empiricism as expressed by Locke and Hume. He felt that empiricism, with its emphasis on sensation, limited the individual's capacity for moral imagination. His own advice was not to translate, collate, distill all the systems, as "it steads you nothing, for truth will not be compelled in any mechanical manner" (1960, p. 272).

Emerson believed that the individual and the universe were connected through a fundamental unity. Emerson (1965) states:

> In the woods, we return to reason and faith. There I feel
> that nothing can befall me in life–no disgrace, no
> calamity (leaving me my eyes), which nature cannot
> repair. Standing on the bare ground–my head bathed
> by the blithe air, on and uplifted into infinite space, all
> mean egotism vanishes. I become a transparent eyeball;
> I am nothing; I see all; the currents of the Universal
> Being circulate through me; I am part or particle of
> God. (p. 189)

We are able to see or apprehend this unity not by sensation but
through intuition. According to Emerson (1965),

> The inquiry leads us to that source, at once the essence
> of genius, the essence of virtue, and the essence of life,
> which we call Spontaneity or Instinct. We denote this
> primary wisdom as Intuition, whilst all later teachings
> are tuitions. In that deep force, the last fact behind
> which analysis cannot go, all things find their common
> origin. (p. 267)

How do we develop this intuition? Emerson believed in the value
of silent contemplation. He liked to take long walks on the trails surrounding Concord. He would then return to his study and record his
thoughts. Emerson kept a journal, the primary source for his lectures
and essays. He read extensively and integrated this reading into his
work; however, he felt the primary inspirational source was the "infinitude" within each person.

For Emerson consciousness was primary, and he sought to deepen
it through meditation and reflection. He looked forward to the time of
"self-union" where he was alone and could simply be with nature and
his own thoughts. In silence the individual could be more receptive to
what he called the Over-Soul, the source of inspiration and creativity.
He (1960) said: "God comes in by a private door into every individual:
thoughts enter by passages which the individual never left open" (vol.
2, p. 250). Again, Emerson loved walking in the Concord area; in the
woods he felt "God was manifest as he surely was not in the sermon"
(vol. 5, pp. 502-503). The thoughts that visit one in solitude have a
mysterious quality:

> Always our thinking is an observing. Into us flows the
> stream evermore of thought from we know not whence.
> We do not determine what we will think; we only open
> our senses, clear away as we can all obstruction from the
> facts, and let God think through us. Then we carry away
> in the ineffaceable memory the result, and all men and
> all the ages confirm it. It is called Truth. (1903, vol. 2,
> pp. 328-329)

The artist and poet are channels "through which streamlets from
the infinite abyss of thought pass into knowledge and use of men"
(1964, vol. 1, p. 226). Emerson felt that by emptying ourselves we see
the truth behind the images of things. He was deeply influenced by
Plato, and he felt that behind the physical world lay a more perfect
spiritual world where the essence of things lay. Through solitude and
quiet we can gain access to this world. However, Emerson does not
create a duality between the physical and the non-visible worlds. The
physical world has its own inherent beauty that reflects the invisible.
Emerson made constant reference to nature as an example. For
example: "the ethereal tides to roll and circulate through him; then he
is caught into the life of the Universe, his speech is thunder, his thought
is law, and his words are universally intelligible as the plants and animals." (1903, vol. 3, p. 26)

According to Gay Wilson Allen, Emerson (1903) also anticipated
thinkers like Fritjof Capra with his insights into nature, as Emerson saw
a connection between matter and energy:

> There is one animal, one planet, one matter and one
> force [that is, energy]. The laws of light and of heat
> translate into each other;—so do the laws of sound and
> of color; and so galvanism, electricity and magnetism
> are varied forms of the self same energy. While the stu-
> dent ponders this immense unity, he observes that all
> things in Nature, the animals, the mountain, the river, the
> seasons, wood, iron, stone, vapor, have a mysterious
> relation to his thoughts and his life; their growths,
> decays, quality, and use so curiously resemble himself
> in parts and in wholes, that he is compelled to speak by
> means of them. (1903, vol. 8, pp. 8-9)

Emerson demonstrates strong insights into the connection between humans and nature. For Emerson, we are not separate from nature but connected in the deepest possible sense.

It is in silence that we have moments of insight and knowing. Emerson (1903) says: "Our faith comes in moments; our vice is habitual. Yet, there is a depth in those brief moments which constrains us to ascribe more reality to them than to all other experiences" (vol. 2, p. 267). Emerson believed that our spontaneous thoughts are our best thoughts and that spontaneous action is our best action.

Of the contemplatives mentioned in this chapter, Emerson is the classic householder. With his wife Lidian he raised three children, lived in one community his whole life, and made his living by writing and lecturing. He served on the Concord school board and attended town meetings. In short, he did not separate himself from society. Yes, he withdrew to the woods to contemplate and reflect, but he always returned to write down his thoughts, which he then shared in his lectures. Despite his life as a family person and member of a small new England community, people were constantly visiting him. One visitor was Moncure Conway from Virginia, who wrote his own biography of Emerson. Emerson took Conway for a walk and ended the day with a visit to Thoreau's hut at Walden, where Thoreau had lived six years earlier.

> At length their steps led them to the ruins of Thoreau's hut, forsaken six summers past. There, not so much for the words spoken as for the power exuded, standing by those visible reminders of a dream that had gone from the particular to the universal, Emerson, in Conway's eyes, seemed for the moment transfigured, "an incarnation of the wondrous day he had given me." Emerson seemed able at will to produce for an aspiring disciple a moment of ecstatic intimacy that grappled that person to him, forever after, with hoops of adamantine. In quest of such experiences men have sought out gurus. A growing number of men could say that while Concord held Emerson men need not travel to the Himalayas. (McAleer, 1984, p. 542)

Many who came in contact with Emerson commented on a certain radiance of being. Nathaniel Hawthorne, who was not a close friend of Emerson though he lived in Concord, said, "A pure intellectual gleam diffused about his presence like the garment of a shining one" (cited in McAleer, p. 426). Hawthorne's wife, Rose, said this:

> It became one of my happiest experiences to pass Emerson upon the street. Yet, I caviled at his self-consciousness, his perpetual smile. I complained that he ought to wait for something to smile at. . . . After a time, I realized that he always had something to smile FOR, if not to smile AT; and that a cheerful countenance is heroic. By and by I learned that he always could find something to smile at also; for he tells us, "The best of all jokes is the sympathetic contemplation of things." (Holmes, 1885, 1980, pp. 238-239)

Another example of the impact the man could have is described by Charles Eliot Norton. Norton was returning to the United States from Europe just after his wife died, and he was quite depressed. Emerson, who was 70 at the time, was on the ship, and the two spent much time together. Initially Norton was put off by Emerson's optimism. Shortly after the trip, however, he wrote his friend James Russell Lowell, "Emerson . . . made the voyage pleasant to me. . . . He had a spirit of perennial youthfulness. He is the youngest man I know" (cited in McAleer, 1984, p. 623). In 1903 Norton paid a centennial tribute to Emerson when he said that Emerson was one of the the most important teachers in his life. He said, "And of these highest inspired men whose acquaintance is beyond price, and who elevate those who come into relations with them by sentiment and habitual grandeur of view, was Emerson himself" (cited in McAleer, 1984, p. 623).

Emerson, in one essay on education, speaks to teachers about the qualities that are fundamental to be an inspiring teacher. He said (1965):

> To whatsoever upright mind, to whatsoever beating heart I speak, to you it is committed to educate men. By simple living, by an illimitable soul, you inspire, you correct, you instruct, you raise, you embellish all. By your own act you teach the beholder how to do the practicable. According to the depth from which you draw your life, such is the depth not only of your strenuous effort but of your manners and presence.

The beautiful nature of the world has here blended your happiness with your power. Work straight on in absolute duty, and you lend an arm and an encouragement to all the youth of the universe. Consent yourself to be an organ of your highest thought, and lo! suddenly you put all men in your debt, and are the fountain of an energy that goes pulsing on waves of benefit to the borders of society, to the circumference of things. (p. 437)

Although he is speaking to teachers, Emerson's words describe his own power as a teacher. His energy, like that of all great teachers, is still "pulsing to the circumference of things."

GANDHI

Gandhi is perhaps the best example of the contemplative involved in social action. Gandhi did not separate his spiritual life from his political activity; for him it was all connected. Gandhi said: "My life is an indivisible whole, and all my activities run into one another" (cited in Easwaran, 1978, p. 5).

Gandhi was born on October 2, 1869, in Porbandar, a small seaside town in western India. His father, Karamchand Gandhi, was a politician who served as prime minister to the raja in the small domains near Porbandar. His mother, Putlibai, was a devout Hindu whom Gandhi remembered as a "deeply religious" person.

As a boy Gandhi was not exceptional except that he was extremely shy. Gandhi, like most Indians, was married at a very early age. At age 13 he married Kasturbai. In his youth he was quite a demanding husband, and the two often fought. However, the marriage endured, in part due to her patience, forbearance, and strong will. At the beginning of the marriage, he saw himself as her teacher, but as the years passed her strength, courage, and patience became a strong example to him and influenced him in the development of satyagraha (soul force) which was his approach to nonviolent change.

Gandhi did not do well in school. After high school he went to college but dropped out after five months. Gandhi's uncle suggested that he go to London to study law, and Gandhi spent three years there, attaining his law degree. When he returned to India, he was devastated to learn that his mother had died. He could not find work as a lawyer because he knew nothing of Indian law and was still very shy. On his first case, he got up to cross-examine, and he could not utter a single word; he was called by his colleagues the "briefless barrister."

There was a major turning point in Gandhi's life when his brother helped him obtain an offer from a local Muslim law firm to work in South Africa. On his first train ride in South Africa, his law firm had reserved him a first-class ticket. In the evening, a white passenger came into his compartment and objected to the presence of a dark-skinned Indian. When the train officials asked Gandhi to move to the third-class section, he refused. He was thrown off the train at the next stop, and he had to spend the cold night at the station. During that evening, Gandhi thought about returning to India but decided that he must stay. Later Gandhi would refer to this incident as the most creative moment in his life. He decided during that long night in the train station that he would never yield to force, nor would he use force to achieve an end. This was the seed that developed into satyagraha many years later.

In South Africa Gandhi was first asked to help with a complicated case that required knowledge of accounting. Gandhi applied himself and was able to attain an out-of-court settlement. He said, "I had learnt to find out the better side of human nature and to enter men's hearts. I realized that the true function of a lawyer was to unite parties riven asunder" (cited in Easwaran, 1978, p. 22). Gandhi's first success led to others, and he became well established as a lawyer. However, after several years there, Gandhi became involved in relieving the suffering of the Indians who lived in South Africa. These people worked as laborers in situations equivalent to slavery. As he witnessed and helped these people, he began to simplify his life; he gave up the expensive clothes and made his household simple. At first he tried to impose this new life on his wife, Kasturbai, who resisted. Her resistance led Gandhi to an important insight; in order to change others you must first change yourself. Gandhi realized that leadership must come from example.

The *Bhavagad Gita* was another powerful influence for Gandhi. He read it daily, and it became his guide for living. He said: "to me the Gita became an infallible guide of conduct. It became my dictionary of daily reference" (Easwaran, 1978, p. 35). The *Gita* also inspired Gandhi to meditate. For the rest of his life, he would rise around 4:00 A.M. and meditate in the quiet of the morning.

In 1906, thirteen years after Gandhi's arrival in South Africa, the white government of Transvaal introduced legislation to take away the few rights the Indians held in South Africa. Gandhi strongly opposed the measure, and he proposed to a crowd that they resist the legislation in a nonviolent manner. He advocated civil disobedience:

> Civil disobedience is the inherent right of a citizen. . . . Disobedience to be civil must be sincere, respectful, restrained, never defiant, must be based upon some well-understood principle, must not be capricious, and above all, must have no ill will or hatred behind it. (Easwaran, 1978, p. 43)

Satyagraha means "holding on to truth" or "soul force." Truth for Gandhi was eternal and unchangeable, while evil and injustice existed only with human support. Once we agreed to hold to the truth, we would become free. Freedom started in our own hearts and minds, and satyagraha was based on individual and collective commitment to holding to truth. Ahimsa, or nonviolence, was the other key element in Gandhi's strategy. Ahimsa and satyagraha are based on the notion that the opponent and the protestor are one; thus one approaches confrontation with deep compassion for the opponent. Gandhi said:

> In satyagraha, it is never the numbers that count; it is always the quality, more so when the forces of violence are uppermost.
> Then it is often forgotten that it is never the intention of a satyagrahi to embarrass the wrongdoer. The appeal is never to his fear; it is, must be, always to his heart. The satyagrahi's object is to convert, not to coerce, the wrongdoer. He should avoid artificiality in all his doings. He acts naturally and from inward conviction. (Easwaran, 1978, p. 53)

His struggle against the South African government and its leader, General Jan Smuts, lasted seven years but in the end was successful, as the hated law, "the Black Act," was overturned. Gandhi and his followers were imprisoned, but through their steadfastness of purpose they won their case.

Gandhi returned to India in 1914. Gradually, he became involved in India's struggles against British domination. He also saw the connection between British control and India's treatment of its own people, particularly the untouchables. Gandhi called these people Harijans, or children of God, and called on Indians to end their cruel treatment of these people. He said: "All of us are one. When you inflict suffering on others, you are bringing suffering on yourself. When you weaken others, you are weakening yourself, weakening the whole nation" (cited in Easwaran, 1978, p. 56). Gandhi refused to go into temples where the Harijans were excluded. He said to the crowds, "There is no God here. If God were here, everyone would have access. He is in every one of us" (Easwaran, 1978, p. 59). As a result of Gandhi's campaign, many places that were once off limits to the untouchables opened their doors.

Again Gandhi taught from example. He traveled third class on the train, went to live with the Harijans, and helped them improve their health and sanitation procedures. His followers did the same.

Gandhi drew many to the cause of nonviolent resistance against the British. One of the most famous followers was Jawaharlal Nehru. Nehru came from a wealthy Indian family, and after meeting Gandhi he gave up his expensive lifestyle and put his energy and wealth into Gandhi's movement. Nehru's father, Motilal, was very upset by this and went to Gandhi pleading to him to give him his son back. In exchange, Motilal would give Gandhi money in support of the movement for independence. Gandhi replied, "Not only do I want your son, I want you, and your wife, and your daughters, and the rest of your family too" (Easwaran, 1978, p. 65). The entire family did become members of Gandhi's movement, starting with Motilal himself. Gandhi, as a personal presence, had a powerful effect on people. His warmth and humor were infectious. Even British administrators were warned to stay away from Gandhi or they too would become converts to the movement.

Gandhi was a formidable opponent because his actions were so unpredictable. Eknath Easwaran, in *Gandhi the Man* (1978), states, "Every move he made was spontaneous; every year that passed found him more youthful, more radical, more experimental. . . . No one knew what he was going to do next, for his actions were prompted not by stale calculations of what seemed politically expedient, but by a deep intuition" (p. 65). These intuitions often came to Gandhi in meditation, or sometimes in his dreams.

Gandhi's behavior is a good example of Emerson's belief that the spontaneous action is the best action. There is more likelihood that this action will be in harmony with the Way, or the natural order of things.

Gandhi's salt march is one of the best examples of spontaneous action. In 1930 the campaign for independence had reached a crucial point when the Indian Congress party raised the flag of freedom as a signal of a new era in the struggle for independence. India was very tense waiting for either side to make a move. Gandhi was expected to provide leadership, and he withdrew to his ashram to meditate. For weeks he sat quietly, while those around him urged him to act. Finally, the answer came to Gandhi in a dream. The British had passed a law that made it illegal for anyone in India to make their own salt. Gandhi saw that this was a perfect example of how the British exploited India. He felt that the best way to confront the British was to march to the sea and take some salt from the water there. This was the famous salt march.

Gandhi started with 78 of his followers and walked 12 miles each day for 24 days. Gandhi was 61 at the time, yet he walked briskly and energetically for the entire length of the march. When Gandhi reached the water, a huge crowd had gathered to watch him as he took a small bit of salt from the sand. Immediately, huge crowds along the coastline gathered salt and then sold it in the cities. As a result, thousands of Indians were arrested and imprisoned, while many others were beaten and killed by the police. Throughout, however, the Indians maintained their peaceful protest. For a long period Gandhi remained free, but finally the police came and arrested him at his ashram. When he went to prison, there were 60,000 satyagrahri in jail. Gandhi, of course, was imprisoned several times during his life. He used his time there to pray, meditate, read, and answer his mail. Many people have seen the salt march as the defining moment in the move to eventual independence for India. Louis Fischer (1954), in his biography of Gandhi, says:

> The Salt March and its aftermath did two things: it gave the Indians the conviction that they could lift the foreign yoke from their shoulders; it made the British aware that they were subjugating India. It was inevitable, after 1930, that India would some day refuse to be ruled, and more important, that England would some day refuse to rule.
>
> When the Indians allowed themselves to be beaten with batons and rifle butts and did not cringe, they showed that England was powerless and India invincible. The rest was merely a matter of time. (p. 102)

Of course, independence did come to India after World War II, but not in the way Gandhi envisioned. India was divided into Hindu India and Muslim Pakistan, and in the process thousands of people died. Gandhi fasted to help curtail the violence in Calcutta. Another burden he faced at the end of his life was the death of Kasturbai in 1944. He deeply grieved her loss.

Gandhi was assassinated by a Hindu fanatic who was upset at Gandhi's influence by means of the fast in Calcutta. When Gandhi was shot, his only words were "Rama," the Indian name for God.

Gandhi's main form of meditation throughout his life was mantra, as he constantly repeated the word "Rama" over and over. Gandhi had been taught this mantra when he was young by a family servant, Rambha. The mantra was a constant source of strength for Gandhi throughout his struggles. Gandhi stated, "The mantram becomes one's staff of life and carries one through every ordeal. . . . Each repetition . . . has a new meaning, each repetition carries you nearer and nearer to God" (cited in Easwaran, 1978, p. 117)

Gandhi found that the mantra of Rama made him joyful. As he walked or worked he repeated it to himself. If Gandhi was involved in struggles that could produce anger and feelings of ill will, he found that the mantra settled his mind. As Easwaran (1978) comments: "Over the years, as the mantram penetrated below his deepest doubts and fears, he became established in joy" (p.118). Gandhi felt that you gradually become what you meditate on. If we meditate on God, then we become part of God. For Gandhi, meditation was a means of reuniting with the source.

Besides the mantra, Gandhi meditated on the *Bhavagad Gita*. He particularly liked the second chapter. Gandhi felt that the verses of the second chapter were inscribed on his heart.

Gandhi was once asked to give a message to his people. He wrote on a small piece of paper, "My life is my message" (cited in Easwaran, 1978, p. 140). Everything Gandhi did was a contemplative act. Easwaran (1978) says in his biography of Gandhi, "To those who met him, even many who came as enemies, he was the supreme artist who had made the smallest detail of his life a work of art" (p. 125). Despite the fact that Gandhi had become a world figure whose activity affected the course of millions in India, he gave complete attention to every detail of his life. Through loving attention he transformed himself, those around him, and eventually an entire nation. Easwaran (1978) has claimed, "Historians of the future, I believe, will look upon this century not as the atomic age, but as the age of Gandhi" (p. 5). Gandhi is our best example how contemplation can be applied to social action.

MERTON

Thomas Merton, the Catholic Trappist monk, made important connections between Christian and Buddhist forms of contemplation. He is certainly one of the most important contemplatives of this century.

Merton was born on January 31, 1915, in Paris. His mother, Ruth, was American, and he remembered her as a "slight, thin, sober little person with a serious and somewhat anxious face" (1948, p. 117). In Merton's view she was also rather "cerebral." His father, Owen, was from New Zealand and was an artist who painted landscapes with watercolors.

Merton's mother died from stomach cancer when he was 6 years old. Merton (1948) recalled: "A tremendous weight of sadness and depression settled on me. It was not the grief of a child, with pangs of sorrow and many tears. It had something of the heavy perplexity and gloom of adult grief, and was therefore all the more of a burden because it was, to that extent, unnatural" (p. 20). His mother's death made his childhood insecure, and he also held some bitter feelings about his mother; later in life he stated "perhaps solitaries are made by severe mothers" (Furlong, p. 15).

Merton spent most of his early childhood in the New York area. However, in 1924 his father moved to France. Although Merton was upset by the move, his years in France were important. Rural France and the Catholic culture appealed to Merton, and he felt very much at home there, although he was unhappy at school. Three years later he and his father moved to England. After living a few years there, Merton suffered the loss of his father. Thus, as a young teenager Merton found himself without parents, and his godparents became his guardians.

Merton went to Oakham Public School in England and did well, particularly in the languages. Before going to university at Cambridge, he had his first profound spiritual experience. Merton had a vision of his father that seemed very real and led to an immediate sense of inadequacy and a need for spiritual connection. He wrote (1948), "And now I think for the first time in my whole life I really began to pray . . . praying out of the very roots of my life and of my being, and praying to the God I had never known, to reach down towards me out of His darkness" (p. 114).

Merton studied one year at Cambridge, but it was a disaster. He did not do well in school, and he also fathered a child. Guilt arose not only from this event but also from the fact that he did not keep in touch with the child or the mother, who were both to die in an air raid in London during World War II.

Merton decided to move to the United States and study at Columbia. At Columbia he was strongly influenced by one of his professors, Mark Van Doren, who taught English there. Merton (1954) said: "The influence of Mark's sober and sincere intellect, and his manner of dealing with his subject with perfect honesty and objectivity and without evasions, was remotely preparing my mind to receive the good seed of scholastic philosophy" (pp. 141-142).

It was also at Columbia that Merton decided to become a Catholic. Some of Merton's close friends at Columbia were spiritually oriented and supported Merton's own spiritual inclinations. Merton (1948) describes his own decision.

> Suddenly, I could bear it no longer. I put down the book, and got into my raincoat, and started down the stairs. I went out into the street. I crossed over, and waslked along by the grey wooden fence, towards Broadway, in the light rain.
>
> And then everything inside me began to sing. I had nine blocks to walk. Then I turned the corner of 121st Street, and the brick church and presbytery were before me. I stood in the doorway and rang the bell and waited. When the maid opened the door I said:
>
> "May I see Father Ford, please?"
>
> "But Father Ford is out."
>
> The maid closed the door. I stepped back into the street. And then I saw Father Ford coming around the corner from Broadway. . . . I went to meet him and said:
>
> "Father may I speak to you about something?"
>
> "Yes," he said, looking up, surprised. "Yes, sure, come into the house."
>
> We sat in the little parlor by the door. And I said:
>
> "Father, I want to become a Catholic." (pp. 212-213)

His Columbia friends attended his first Communion. Although Merton still went to wild student parties and had affairs with girls, from the moment of his conversion he was a devoted Catholic. He went to Mass often, more than once a week, and regularly went to confession and Communion. He also learned the rosary and did a lot of spiritual reading. But he still was confused. One of his close friends, Bob Lax, said to him once, while they were walking down Sixth Avenue in New York, that the only important task in life was to be a saint and all you had to do was want it badly enough. Merton went to Mark Van Doren and asked if this was true, and Van Doren agreed. Merton wondered why his non-Christian friends such as Lax, who was Jewish, could see things so clearly.

Merton finished his M.A. and began writing a novel. While living the life of a struggling writer, one day while with friends, the thought entered his mind, "I am going to be a priest." He told his friends, and they thought it was another temporary enthusiasm. However, from this moment Merton's life began to change; he gave up the wild parties, girls, and drinking. He went to a Franciscan monastery in New York to see if he could join, but they told him he had to wait, because applicants were only accepted once a year. His application, however, was rejected when he told a Franciscan of his past. Merton was crushed by the rejection, but he did not give up his desire to go to a monastery.

In what he felt was the important year of his life–1941–Merton went to a retreat at the Trappist Monastery, Gethsemani, in Kentucky. When he arrived there, he immediately felt at home and wondered again whether he might be able to become a monk. In a brief conversation with Mark Van Doren, Van Doren asked whether he still wanted to be a monk and encouraged him to go ahead with his idea of becoming a priest. Merton seized upon this encouragement and decided to go to Gethsemani again for a Christmas retreat. When he arrived there, he applied to be a postulant and was accepted.

The life at Gethsemani was hard. There was no heating or air conditioning, and the monks were expected to do a great deal of manual labor. Silence was the rule; the monks could speak only to their superiors. The monks used signs to communicate. The food was vegetarian, and according to Merton, it was not well cooked and was tasteless. The monks rose at 2:00 A.M. and retired at 7:00 P.M. and during the waking hours, the day was structured around work and prayer.

Merton found that the simple life at Gethsemani sharpened his awareness and brought him closer to God. In these beginning years as a monk, Merton equated contemplation with concentration. According to Michael Mott (1984), "He learned to concentrate entirely on what he was doing, on his prayer, his reading, his writing." The ability to see with the concentrated eye was to make his writing more detailed and much richer in effect. Merton recalled the two years as a novice monk as a very happy period in his life. The monastery provided a home and structure that he had missed for most of his life.

However, near the end of his initial training, about two years after his arrival at Gethsemani, Merton reached a state of collapse. Part of this was sheer physical exhaustion because of the difficult routine at Gethsemani, but some of it may have also been due to the fact that Merton's desire to write was not being met. He discussed this need with his superiors, and they decided to support his writing if it dealt with Trappist life. This approval eventually led to *The Seven Storey Mountain*. This autobiography, which describes Merton's spiritual path to Catholicism and Gethsemani, became a worldwide best-seller. The original hardback sold 600,000 copies. The book made Merton famous, and he began to receive voluminous mail from around the world.

Merton also wrote *The Seeds of Contemplation* in the late forties. Some consider this Merton's best description of the contemplative life. It is not a how-to book, but describes Merton's approach within the Catholic monastic tradition. Merton's definition of contemplation, which was cited in the first chapter of this book, is found in the updated version of the book, *New Seeds of Contemplation*.

Life at Gethsemani was often a struggle for Merton. He often felt constrained by his superiors and the life in general. His occasional feelings of anger at his superiors reinforced a sense of guilt.

Merton became the person responsible for teaching, first, as the master of scholastics, and then as the master of novices. Although he enjoyed teaching immensely, this was another activity that made him tired. His overwork and conflicts would lead to periodic sickness, when he would have to retire to the infirmary. In 1950, while he was in the infirmary, he saw the importance of solitude. He wrote: "Solitude is not found so much by looking outside the boundaries of your dwelling, as by staying within. Solitude is not something you must hope for in the future. Rather, it is a deepening of the present, and unless you look for it in the present you will never find it" (cited in Furlong, 1980, p. 178).

Throughout his life Merton saw the need for quiet and solitude, not only for himself but for others as well. He once wrote in the 1950s, "Provide people with places where they can go to be quiet—relax minds and hearts in the presence of God. . . . Reading rooms, hermitages. Retreat houses without a constant ballyhoo of noisy 'exercises'" (cited in Furlong, 1980, p. 186). Merton's vision has become more of a reality in the 1990s, for retreat centers of various kinds have arisen all over North America.

The search for solitude led to Merton's desire for privacy at Gethsemani. Merton's writing had attracted new monks to the order and the monastery had become overcrowded. He wrote (1954), "The cloister is as crowded as a Paris street" (cited in Furlong, 1980, p. 203).

Merton dreamed of being a hermit. Around this time, one of his books, *The Sign of Jonas,* was not approved by the church for publication. Merton wanted to transfer to an Italian monastery where the monks were almost entirely alone, but his request was thwarted.

In the midfifties Merton became a teacher of the novice monks. He enjoyed teaching, and by all accounts was an extremely effective teacher. One former student recalls his impressions of Merton:

> The first time I saw him he was bouncing down the cloister, making all the signs we weren't supposed to make, and which he bawled us out for making. We were all going into the church and he was going in the opposite direction which I suppose was a part of the joke. He never wanted you to take him too seriously. Everybody loved him. Some of the monks might think some of his ideas were wild, but he was much loved. You couldn't look up to him as an elder except in his spiritual teaching and his direction. (Furlong, 1980, p. 219)

During the fifties Merton came to terms with himself. He did not care so much about being the "good" monk, and he became more comfortable with himself. By the late fifties he was reading widely in many areas. He also ventured into literature from Eastern religions. By the early 1960s, Merton had become intensely interested in the issues of the day such as civil rights and the threat of nuclear war. He was corresponding with people about these issues, and many people came to see him at Gethsemani. Merton was also allowed to go to New York to see the Zen master D. T. Suzuki, who was interested in Merton's work.

The 1960s also saw one of Merton's dreams come true, as he was able to have his own hermitage, or small house, separate from the monastery. The hermitage brought him closer to nature, and he enjoyed watching his surroundings and feeling a part of them. He even had a record player, and he particularly enjoyed the music of Mozart. Many people who met Merton were struck by his personal presence.

For example, the Indonesian ambassador to Washington, Dr. Soedjatmaoko (1970) wrote:

> If there is one impression that has stayed with me all along it is a memory of one of the very few people I have known in this world with an inner freedom which is almost total. It was, I felt, an inner freedom which was not negative, in terms of something else, but it was like the water that constantly flows out of a well. (Cited in Mott, 1984, p. 535)

One person saw Merton as a "living example of the freedom and transformation of consciousness which meditation can give." Near the end of his life, Merton (1968) looked at contemplation in the following manner:

> Duty of the contemplative life–(Duty's the wrong word)–to provide an area, a space of liberty, of silence, in which possibilities are allowed to surface and new choices–beyond routine choice–become manifest. To create a new experience of time, not as stoppage, stillness, but as "temps vierge"–not a blank to be filled or an untouched space to be conquered and violate, but to enjoy its own potentialities and hopes and its own presence to itself. One's *own* time (Not dominated by one's ego and its demands), hence open to others–*compassionate* time. (pp. 68-69)

This has much the flavor of Emerson's spontaneous thoughts. Near the end of his life, Merton wrote the following: "Our real journey in life is interior; it is a matter of growth, deepening, and of ever greater surrender to creative action of love and grace in our hearts" (cited in Mott, p. 543).

Merton died unexpectedly while he was in Asia in 1968. Shortly before his death, he spoke to a group of people representing different faiths in Calcutta. The words are at the heart of Merton's (1975) view of contemplation:

> And the deepest level of communication is not communication, but communion. It is wordless. It is beyond words, and it is beyond speech, and it is beyond

concept. Not that we discover a new unity. We discover an older unity. My dear brothers, we are already one. But we imagine that we are not. And what we have to recover is our original unity. What we have to be is what we are. (p. 307)

Many people today find Merton an inspiring figure for their own practice. Particularly important from my perspective is his ability to explore contemplative practices from other traditions (e.g., Buddhism) and connect these to his own Christian tradition. As we move to the twenty-first century, this ability to connect contemplative traditions will become even more significant.

SUMMARY

The five contemplatives outlined here are different in many ways. For example, each had a unique approach to meditation. The Buddha focused on awareness of the breath and becoming mindful in daily life.

Teresa of Avila's approach to contemplation was within a Christian monastic framework. Despite this focus, her numerous descriptions of meditative practice have a universal quality. She describes both the context and the stages of contemplative practice in a detailed yet accessible manner. Her life also shows that contemplation can be a tremendous source of energy, as she founded seventeen Carmelite convents and was an incredibly active force in the religious life of Spain in the sixteenth century.

Emerson's approach to contemplation was less formal. When I take a walk, I think of Emerson, who said, "Think me not unkind and rude that I walk alone in grove and glen; I go to the God of the wood to fetch His word to men." By being present in nature, Emerson teaches how we can become nourished and renewed. Emerson's use of the journal is also instructive, as keeping a journal can be a contemplative act. When our thoughts and reflections arise spontaneously, the journal allows us to record the thoughts and images. Emerson shows how contemplation can be part of our life in a way that energizes us and also lets us connect with others in our family, our neighborhood, and our community. Although Emerson contemplated in nature, he always came back to share his thoughts with others through his lectures and writing and by his simple presence.

Gandhi connected meditation with conscious social action. He showed how to approach change in a way that is in harmony with the way things are. He realized that when we try to change things from the perspective of the ego, we eventually cause more suffering. However, through contemplation, we can see more deeply into the true nature of things, and our efforts to bring about change in our institutions and society will be more fulfilling. Often our efforts to change our environment let us fall into a we-they scenario, and Gandhi taught us how a contemplative approach lets us see everyone as "we."

Merton, the most contemporary of the contemplatives, was also the most reclusive, since he pursued the monastic life. Yet he struck a chord with so many individuals that his work is relevant to all who seek contemplative life, no matter what the outer circumstances. Merton's life demonstrates that one can keep learning and growing in the contemplative life. Although committed to Catholic practice, his interest in Buddhism toward the end of his life shows how we can connect contemplative practices across different paths. He shows that, ultimately, there is a unity behind the various practices. This unity comes out in the being of each person described here. Buddha, Teresa of Avila, Emerson, Gandhi, and Merton were warm, loving, and spontaneous individuals. They show us how contemplation allows us to live life more fully—with more directness, purpose, and joy. They are a constant reminder of the ultimate fruits of the contemplative life.

REFERENCES

Allen, G. W. (1981). *Waldo Emerson.* New York: Viking Press.

Conway, M. D. (1882). *Emerson at home and abroad.* Boston: Houghton Mifflin.

Easwaran, E. (1978). *Gandhi the man.* Berkeley, CA: Nilgiri Press.

Emerson, R. W. (1903). *The complete works.* Ed. Edward Emerson. 12 vols. Boston: Houghton Mifflin.

——. (1964-72) *Early lectures of Ralph Waldo Emerson.* Ed. S. E. Whicher, R. E. Spiller, & W. E. Williams. 3 vols. Cambridge: Harvard University Press.

——. (1960-78). *The journals and miscellaneous notebooks of Ralph Waldo Emerson.* Ed. W. Gillman et al. Vols. 1-14. Cambridge: Harvard University Press .

——. (1965). *Selected Writings.* Ed. W. H. Gilman. New York: New American Press.

Fischer, L. (1954). *Gandhi: His life and message for the world*. New York: Mentor.

Flinders, C. L. (1993). *Enduring grace: Living portraits of seven women mystics*. San Francisco: Harper/San Francisco.

Furlong, M. (1980). *Merton: A biography*. New York: Harper

Holmes, O. W. (1885, 1980). *Ralph Waldo Emerson*. Boston: Houghton Mifflin.

McAleer, J. (1984). *Ralph Waldo Emerson: Days of encounter*. Boston: Little, Brown and Company.

Merton, T. (1948). *The seven storey mountain*. New York: Signet Books.

——. (1968). Asian notes. Unpublished.

——. (1972). *New Seeds of Contemplation*. New York: New Directions.

——. (1975). *The Asian journal of Thomas Merton*. New York: New Directions.

Mott, M. (1984). *The seven mountains of Thomas Merton*. Boston: Houghton Mifflin.

Ross, N. W. (1980). *Buddhism: A way of life and thought*. New York: Knopf.

Teresa of Avila. (1946). *The collected works*. 3 vols. Trans. & Ed. E. A. Peers. London: Sheed & Ward.

6

Contemplative Practice in Higher Education

Higher education in North America is under attack. Ernest Boyer, ex-chancellor of the State University of New York, argues that universities have lost "their sense of mission," for they suffer a paralysis in the definition of the "essential purposes and goals" (cited in de Nicolas, 1989, p. 9). One of the most interesting critiques comes from Antonio T. de Nicolas (1989) in his book *Habits of Mind*. De Nicolas argues that the university is dominated by the culture of technology, or the "instrumentation of reason; that is, it makes of reason an instrument to achieve quantitative efficiency; . . . universities become centres for the production, transmission, and storage of information" (p. 13).

De Nicolas (1989) proposes a curriculum that focuses on developing habits of mind. He argues that these habits must go beyond scientism and include those suggested by Plato in his dialogues and in *The Republic*. These habits include:

> the abstraction of images from objects already in the world, the forming of opinions, cognitive operations with their diverse levels of abstraction as exemplified in the operations of science and art, and the whole range of imaginative operations for original creation without borrowing from the outside, by recollecting from the past those memories of images, and acts that represent the best of what is human and cultural. (de Nicolas, 1989, p. xvii)

De Nicolas teaches a course to undergraduates in which students perform an enactment of the philosophy they have studied. This encourages the students to immerse themselves in various habits of mind. In the case of Plato, some of these habits border on the mystical. De Nicolas (1989) cites Plato's *Phaedo*, where the soul learns to "withdraw from all contact with the body and concentrate itself on itself . . . alone by itself" (p. 46). What is interesting is that de Nicolas is referring to contemplation, but he never includes it as one of the habits. In sum, de Nicolas offers an interesting critique and proposals for change; yet I find his vision incomplete.

It is the contemplation that goes beyond subjective object duality (see chapter 2) that I find missing in de Nicolas's conception. Contemplation clearly goes beyond reflection, inquiry, and logic to the point where the person is not thinking *about* or reflecting *on* something but in some sense has become part of what he or she sees.

A RATIONALE FOR CONTEMPLATION IN HIGHER EDUCATION

Given this conception of contemplation, why should it have a role in higher education? One important reason is that contemplation is basically a form of Self-learning. Through the process of contemplation, one learns to trust one's own deeper intuitive responses. For example, insight meditation, a form of contemplation, is based on the notion that we can learn and grow by simply mindfully watching our own experience. As we notice our own thoughts and agendas, we can gain deeper insight into ourselves and the nature of experience. In contrast, the model for most learning at the university level is that the professor and the text are the authority and the student must learn from these authorities. Contemplation provides one alternative to this model by recognizing that we can learn from ourselves and our own experience.

Another reason for engaging in contemplation is that it allows students to deal with the stresses in their lives. Research indicates that meditation is an effective tool in the relaxation process (Benson, 1976), and given the pressures that students face today, this aspect of contemplation should not be overlooked. The vast majority of students in my classes have seen the positive effects of contemplative practice, such as having fewer headaches and simply being able to address stressful events that come up in their lives. One of my students is a secondary school vice principal who faces many stressful events during the day. He wrote in his journal that as the pressures of his job increase he finds the "need *to engage in meditation more frequently. During quieter, less hectic times, meditation became more a luxury than a necessity.*"

Perhaps the most important reason for bringing contemplation into the curriculum is that it allows the individual to gradually overcome his or her sense of separateness. Our society reinforces the personal ego, which spends most of the day planning, striving, and competing. Our ego arises from the various social roles we engage in, such as parent, worker, and spouse. The extent that we identify with these roles is also the extent of our suffering. For example, if people invest their whole identity in their work (e.g., the workaholic), they find it extremely difficult to adjust when they retire. The father who is too attached to his role as father may have a difficult time letting go of his son or daughter when he or she leaves home. Almost every spiritual tradition focuses on letting go of ego and letting our Self, Atman, or Buddha-Nature naturally arise.

The social structure we live in continually reinforces the ego through competition and fear. Thus, we constantly are trying to gain an edge on others in our work, on the highway, or when we stand in line at the post office or the grocery store. Meditation lets us witness the striving of the ego. During meditation practice, we compassionately witness all our thoughts and ego trips, and very gradually we begin to see that our fundamental identity is not the thoughts that form our ego structure, but the clear awareness that is witnessing the arising and falling of all of this. This basic insight is the beginning of liberation and compassion.

This last reason is also important to the basic population that I work with, which includes experienced teachers at the elementary and secondary levels. If teaching is ego based, it can become a frustrating series of mini-battles with students. The classroom becomes focused around the issue of control. If we teach from our Self, teaching becomes a fulfilling and enriching experience. Robert Griffin (1977) summarizes this very well:

> You don't feel set off against them [the students] or
> competitive with them. You see yourself in students and
> them in you. You move more easily, are more relaxed,
> seem less threatening to students. You are less
> compulsive, less rigid in your thoughts and actions.

>You aren't so tense. You don't seem to be in a grim
>win-or-lose contest when teaching. (p. 79)

I have elaborated on Self-based teaching in other contexts (Miller,
1981; Drake and Miller, 1991).

CONTEMPLATION IN THE CLASSROOM

I have been practicing vipassana, or insight meditation, since 1974.
My current professional focus is in the area of holistic education, and I
work at the Ontario Institute for Studies in Education. I work with
boards of education trying to bring holistic education into the schools,
and I also teach courses at the graduate level to teachers and school
administrators. One course is entitled "The Holistic Curriculum" and
the other is called "The Teacher as Contemplative Practitioner." In both
these courses I require my students to do some form of contemplation.
The requirement is based on the premise that teaching should come
from the Self rather than the ego. Ego-based teaching ultimately
reinforces our sense of separateness and suffering. I emphasize that
when we teach from the Self, we gradually experience more moments
of communion with our students. Through meditation, we experience
moments of deep inner joy in teaching as we connect with our students
in profound and subtle ways. Holistic education can be defined in
many ways. One definition I like is simply the release of the human
heart. Meditation is fundamental to that release.

Students are introduced to four or five different types of meditation, including meditation on the breath, mantra, visualization, and
concentration on poetry or sacred texts. Some students work out their
own forms. Although I encourage sitting meditation, some of my students do movement meditation. For example, one of my students swam
every day, and he approached swimming from a meditative stance.
Whatever form students choose, I emphasize that in meditation we let
go of the calculating mind and open to the listening mind, which tends
to be characterized by a relaxed alertness. Once the students have
settled on a method, I encourage them to work up to about 30 minutes
a day of meditation practice. I keep in touch with each student through
a journal they keep on their practice. I also introduce students to the
Buddhist lovingkindness meditation in which thoughts of well-being
are sent to oneself and others. I start each class with this meditation and

encourage students to begin or end their own individual meditation with it.

Meditation has been a part of "The Holistic Curriculum" course since 1988, and approximately 400 students have participated. The average enrollment for "The Holistic Curriculum" is around twenty students. The course has always been full, with a number of students on a waiting list. Only one student has asked not to do the meditation assignment, as she had been sexually abused a year before and did not feel comfortable with the practice. I have yet to have a student who has had an overall negative experience with the practice. Most of my students come from Ontario, but I have had students from Brazil, China, Indonesia, Jamaica, Kenya, and Malta.

In the rest of this chapter, I will describe some of the experiences of the students as reported in their journals. Students keep daily journals on their practice, and this is the main vehicle for communicating about how the meditation is going. I will begin with the experiences of one student, as they are typical for many of my students, and then report on certain themes that appear in the students' journals.

A Typical Student's Experience

Jane, an experienced teacher, is working on a doctoral degree at OISE. I believe her meditation experience is typical of that of many of my students. Like other students, she began the practice with some reluctance and difficulty. For example, on her third day of meditating she reported:

> *I'm trying to learn how to do this, and I sense that I need to learn to relax, but it's not something that's coming easily to me! In fact, I suspect I'm trying too hard and defeating the purpose.*

Trying too hard is very common to students. Another student in the beginning said, *"I seem to be fighting for control."*

After a couple of weeks, Jane began to experience some positive benefits from her practice.

> *I'm surprised at how busy my mind is. So many thoughts fight for attention. I'm also having to sort out*

some disturbing emotional issues. It seems that after a time of meditation, I am more relaxed and I feel healthier emotionally, but also more fragile in a sense too.

Yet frustration was still part of her experience.

I can't seem to relax easily. I'm reminded of a photo taken of me when I was only nine months old; even then my fists were clenched . . . am definitely task-oriented, and my self-esteem is tightly wound up in that.

Many of my students share this task orientation. Meditation is so different, because it really reverses the whole notion of trying to achieve something immediate and specific. One way to look at meditation is that it is simply being present in the moment, which runs counter to the whole concept of striving to achieve a specific task or objective.

Initially, Jane did a visualization where she saw herself on "*an empty beach where there are footprints, but the shore is deserted. The sky is blue and there is a cool breeze, rather like early autumn or late spring.*" She sees herself as "*alone, but not lonely*" and she enjoys "*the sights and sounds of waves rolling in*" as she makes her way down the beach. As time went on, she focused more on attending to the rising and falling of the breath rather than the visualization.

After five weeks, Jane began to notice that meditation was having a positive effect on her life. She was studying for comprehensive doctoral exams ("comps") and noticed the effects on her studying

My ability to concentrate on my work after meditating seems greater. Getting closer to "comps" and such, my ability to retain what I'm reading, I feared was diminishing. But today I noticed an alertness, an attention to my work, which I began after meditating. I'm hesitant to link the two as cause-effect, but I'm going to see if there is a pattern here.

Jane's attitude or approach to meditation is one of inquiry; she simply tries to see what patterns emerge from her practice. This is in keeping with the spirit of meditation practice, which tends to be watchful and oriented toward self-inquiry.

Around the eighth week, Jane begins to consider the possibility of continuing her meditation practice after the course is over. She writes:

> *The surprise for me is that I'm beginning to consider the possibility that I might actually continue this practice after the course. Not that I'm a skeptical person, but I just wasn't getting much out of it until very recently. It always seemed to work against my "intense," busy nature and lifestyle. I'm now beginning to see the benefits and to appreciate the difference it might make in my daily life.*

The next day, Jane writes:

> *The irony is that meditation may be something that fits who I am after all. I like this focused, relaxed feeling. . . . This is not what I expected at all.*

After a couple of months, Jane was meditating about 30 minutes a day. She writes about how meditation allows her to transcend the "nonsense" in her life.

> *Now when I have difficulty at the beginning of the meditation, sometimes even into ten minutes or so, I just keep with it. I can now "work through" the initial difficulty of blocking out noises and tension. I now know what the benefits are if one perseveres. There is also a wonderful feeling of getting beyond the busyness and of feeling detached from the nonsense. It's giving me a new way for viewing my daily activities.*

I ask my students to write their summary reflections at the end of the course. One of the interesting points that Jane makes is the following:

> *I'm no longer doing meditation because I sense that "it will be good for me," although I'm convinced that this may be true. Instead, I find myself looking forward to it*

*and looking for times in my day when I'll be able to do
it in addition to my morning session.*

I believe Jane's experience is a common one in my course. At the
beginning there is resistance, frustration, and anger. Gradually, however, for the vast majority of students, there comes a turning point, and
then meditation is no longer filled with frustration but becomes something to which the student looks forward. For some students, the turning point can be a simple insight. One woman noted:

*There were a few frustrating days at this point when I
felt like giving up–I wasn't getting anywhere. But then I
decided there was nowhere to get to, no place I had to
be!*

Another person was having a lot of difficulty getting started. She
wanted to keep herself under tight control during meditation, but this
led to frustration. One day, however, she wrote:

*I didn't intend to meditate at the symphony but I
learned something in the course of the evening. The
second selection was a Bach Concerto for Two Violins.
It started with a vigorous "Vivace" and then switched
to a "Largo," I noticed that my breathing altered sub-
stantially from one section to the other and found
myself breathing slowly during the Largo. The meditation seemed to flow easily. I wasn't following the music
as much as the rhythm. That's when I realized that
meditation, for me anyway, should not be a matter of
control, but rather rhythm.*

I noticed in 1991 that my course drew a few people who had been
meditating for ten or fifteen years. These people were helpful to
beginners who were experiencing difficulties. We met in small groups,
and the experienced practitioners offerred support and helpful advice
to others who were beginning. The advice of the experienced meditator
can also provide the "turning point" for the new student. One student
said:

*Discussion at class last night really helped. Apparently
I'm trying too hard. Two classmates who are experi-*

enced in meditation seem so relaxed about it and recommended letting the thoughts fly by, rather than stopping to judge and resent them.

Themes from the Journals

My students have settled into the process of meditation, and a number of themes seem to emerge from their practice. One theme for many students is that meditation practice provides them with the *permission to be alone* and to enjoy their own company. One teacher said:

As a relaxing strategy it [meditation] has offered a time to get to know me better and to understand me and why I do the things that I do and that most importantly that I am OK. I am an important person for me to get to know and to spend time with. It is a time that I enjoy and have come to need. . . . A time to be with me with no one making demands or needing assistance. I have come to need these minutes to myself.

Another student compared the need to enjoy her own company with teaching kids to like themselves:

We are always talking about having the children like themselves but we do not talk about adults liking themselves and enjoying their own company.

For this student, meditation was an experience in which she learned to accept herself more completely.

A second theme that emerges is that many students feel they become better *listeners* through meditation. One student reported:

Perhaps the most important result has been the evolution of my listening habits. I had thought that I was a pretty attentive, active listener; but I have really extended my ability, or my need, to hear what people are saying.

Another person whose grandfather was sick noted, *"I feel it [meditation] has helped me be more calm and centered, and thus, more able to be present for my mother and cope better with the stress and hardship of my grandfather's illness."*

Finally, another student noticed that he began listening to his body more. He stated in his journal, *"I am listening more to my body and its signals, telling me to become more active about its well-being."*

Related to listening, a third theme that emerges is that people are able to *witness their own lives* from a larger perspective. One student stated:

> *Because I tend to worry a lot, I feel the meditation helps me keep things in perspective and gives me an opportunity to detach myself from my own "melo-drama" and regain a sense of balance and perspective.*

Another student put it this way:

> *I have become aware in a very non threatening manner of the EGO. Because I am alone with my EGO, and not being judged as I work through the process, I am able to ignore my first "knee-jerk" response to an issue and instead delve deeper for understanding and assistance for direction. . . . This is hard . . . but rewarding.*

A fourth theme that arises is that *meditation can happen spontaneously in one's daily life.* One student, for example, noticed that in the stressful place of the dentist's chair, she started to focus on the breath and she then became more centered. Another person found it helpful in his role of father:

> *My son is almost two years old and really hates going to bed. We were visiting my brother and my son was tremendously keyed up and would not go to bed. I hadn't done my meditation yet so I hit upon the brilliant idea of settling him into bed with deep breathing exercises.*
>
> *I brought his bottle in with us (even meditation needs its allies) and turned off the light in his room. I held him in my arms while he cried and squirmed and I slowly (and noisily) began breathing in measured beats. He didn't stop crying immediately but he became*

*very curious with my breathing and his curiosity shifted
to feeling very secure.*

*After some ten minutes I heard him drift off to sleep
and felt his little body relax. I left him in my arms and
proceeded with my meditation in a more relaxed
breathing mode. I simply absorbed the black stillness
around me and listened with pleasure to his quiet little
murmurs.*

A less prominent but still significant theme is that several teachers
have begun to *use meditation in their own classrooms*. Many use
visualization, which is already a popular technique in many classrooms.
One teacher who works in a Catholic secondary school uses meditation
with her students, and reports.

*[Students] ask to meditate and have come to enjoy the
process. They freely admit to not being able to understand the process, and accepting the simple conclusion
that they like the feeling and the results. They have
become "stiller." They can sit for longer periods of time
and their attention span has increased. Students from
other classes that I do not teach have asked to be
taught how to meditate because the other students
claim that they have done better on tests and been in
less trouble. Interesting!!*

*Parents say that students love my classes and really
enjoy the exercises that I do with them. Last night at
parent night they discussed meditation and their child's
reaction. They felt it made their child less aggressive.*

A fifth theme that occurs is the *developing sense of interrelated-
ness and connectedness*. One student wrote in her journal toward the
end of the course:

*I concentrated on my breathing patterns and I slipped
into my familiar stance. Little entered my mind, I was
simply enjoying the sensations of peace and tranquility.
When I awoke, I left the apartment and walked home. I
noticed that I was humming and strolling with a light
step. Children on their bicycles and little puppies in my
path were making me smile. In this remote corner of the*

world, all was calm. I realized after a while that I was mirroring the image of my surroundings and in a small way, it felt wonderful to be a part of the serenity of life.

In essence, I felt that I have participated in an education of introspection, as well as, the experience of interconnectedness with other people, with the surrounding nature, and with the infinite universe.

As mentioned earlier, one of my students applied a meditative awareness to swimming. One day he felt at one with the water. He wrote in his journal, *"The last 20 lengths were euphoric–no discomfort, only a feeling of working together with the water, being strengthened by the water's buoyant force."*

Another student who practiced meditation for many years described his feeling of connectedness this way:

The session began with many thoughts and physical sensations which quickly settled down and although they didn't totally disappear, were not much in my awareness afterward. It was a very quiet and uneventful meditation with the mantra barely present. In fact there was not much present at all except the awareness of myself just being there. This continued until towards the end of the session when I began to have certain feelings or knowledge; it's hard to explain how the two combine into one. It's like you know something with every cell of your body, to the point that you actually feel it everywhere. . . . I was keenly aware that I was part of all that was around me. There was no distinction between my inner self, my body, and my surroundings. This awareness extended out so that I felt a part of all that there is. As I read what I'm writing, the words sound quite grandiose, whereas the experience was very simple. However, it was also profound, peaceful and fulfilling at all levels: physical, intellectual, and spiritual.

Finally, several of my students have pointed out that others begin to notice changes in them. People close to the person see the student as more relaxed and focused. One student wrote:

My wife has noticed a change in my behavior. . . . She pointed out that on the mornings when I meditate I leave for work 5-10 minutes later than my usual 7:30. This is not because I use the extra time for the actual meditation but because I "move slower" as I get ready.

CONCLUSION

At some point meditation practice no longer becomes the 20 or 30 minutes a day that the sitting involves; instead, it infuses one's daily life. Shinzen Young (Tart, 1990) describes this very well:

When you begin your meditation practice, you experience meditation as one of your activities during the day. Somewhere along the line, a figure-ground reversal takes place and you begin to experience all of the activities of the day as happening within meditation. So actually only your body leaves the cushion in the morning, not your consciousness. It seems as though you are literally meditating all day. The events of life are surrounded by a tremendous sense of peace, presence and focus.

In addition to that, you carry with you a basic beneficence that comes through the pores of your being. It influences the people around you, in subtle, if not overt, ways. You feel that every single thing you do, even the most casual activity, is in some way purifying the environment around you. (pp. 164-165)

Some of my students begin to experience this shift in their lives, although perhaps not as profoundly as described by Young. One student described his practice as he went back to work:

Happy with the success of my previous morning meditations, I set the alarm a half hour earlier and climbed into a chair to meditate the next morning.

I was extremely drowsy, bemoaning the fact that one had to work for a living and, I confess, asking myself why was I getting up 30 minutes early to wake

myself up via meditation. I was not a happy camper!
Anyhow, with head barely upright I closed my eyes and
concentrated upon waking up the parts of my body. I
started with my feet because they offered the least resis-
tance, then I slowly woke up my legs, then shoulders
and arms. My head, still the most reluctant, gradually
eased into a quiet and alert state. I settled into this
quiet alertness and let it spread to all parts of my brain.
After 30 minutes of this kind of focused alertness I
opened my eyes and felt very calm and rested and
ready to face the day. As well, this calmness stayed with
me throughout the day.

This student summarizes his experience.

By being more calm and detached I am also more
aware of other people's concerns and priorities. Thus,
ironically, my detachment has facilitated greater unity
and connectedness with those people, issues, and
concerns.

Higher education and teacher education have become departmen-
talized, specialized, and fragmented. Students and professors seem at a
loss as to how to connect information, concepts, and meanings. Most
important, there seems to be a gulf between the subjects and the inner
life of the student. Contemplation is one way to bridge that gulf. It can
allow students to reconnect with their deeper Self and to sort out all
that is happening to them. One of my students wrote in his journal:

I think one of the major flaws of graduate school edu-
cation is that the volume of information "digested"
leaves little time for one to sort out their own connect-
edness to all of this know-ledge. Consequently, the
meditations gave me an opportunity to internalize those
ideas that I thought were worthwhile and reject those
which I felt were superficial.

From my perspective as teacher, the students' reports of their practice in their journals has become a powerful bonding force for student
and teacher. The journals allow me to see students in a much more
complete way. Of course, it is important that teachers be engaged in

their own meditation and that they share thoughts on their practice. In general, I emphasize meditation as a simple, natural activity that can bring clarity and simplicity to our own life.

Although I require meditation in my course, I probably would not do so if the course was required. I believe that students should not be forced into meditation practice. However, there are other courses in which meditation or simply silence could be employed. For example, James Moffett (1981) has argued that meditation can be a vital part of the language arts curriculum. A leading theorist in language education, Moffett suggests, "People who can suspend discourse think and speak better when they turn it back on" (p. 171). Meditation also seems appropriate for arts education. Silence and meditation are often linked with the creative process, and some performers also feel that it enhances their concentration. Even science might find a role for meditation. Einstein, for example, felt that solitude was fundamental to scientific discovery (Clark, 1971). Reform of higher education and teacher education cannot afford to focus on piecemeal change. It must begin to see the whole student, who is not just a vessel to be filled with knowledge or a problem solver but a person, like the rest of us, who also wants to be at home in this universe.

REFERENCES

Benson, H. (1976). *The relaxation response.* New York: Avon.

Bloom, A. (1987). *The closing of the American mind.* New York: Simon & Schuster.

Bodian, S. (1985, May/June). The heart of prayer: An interview with Christian contemplative David Steindl-Rast. *Yoga Journal,* pp. 25-28, 48.

Boyer, E. L. (1987). *College: The undergraduate experience in America.* New York: Harper & Row.

Clark, R. W. (1971). *Einstein: The life and times.* New York: Avon Books

de Nicolas, A. (1989). *Habits of mind: An introduction to the philosophy of education.* New York: Paragon House.

Drake, S. M., & Miller, J. p. (1991) Beyond reflection to being: The contemplative practitioner. *Phenomenology & Pedagogy,* 9, 319-334.

Griffin, R. (1977, February). Discipline: What's it taking out of you? *Learning,* pp. 77-80.

Huxley, A. (1970). *The perennial philosophy*. New York: Harper &
    Row.
Merton, T. (1972). *New seeds of contemplation*. New York: New
    Directions.
Miller, J. (1981). *The compassionate teacher*. Englewood Cliffs, NJ:
    Prentice Hall.
Moffett, J. (1981). Writing, inner speech, and meditation. In J. Moffett,
    (ed.), *Coming on Center*. Montclair, NJ: Boynton/Cook.
Tart, C. (1990). Adapting Eastern spiritual teachings to Western
    culture: A discussion with Shinzen Young. *The Journal of
    Transpersonal Psychology*, 22, pp. 149-166.
Wilber, I. (1983). Eye to eye: The quest for the new paradigm. Garden
    City, NJ: Anchor.

7

The Contemplative Practitioner

In the last chapter I outlined how educators can approach their work from a contemplative perspective. This chapter explores how contemplation can be applied to other fields, such as business, sports, medicine, and the arts. Many of the examples cited in this chapter come from individuals that I have interviewed, although some examples are drawn from the research literature. The second part of the chapter describes different ways that we can begin to slow down. Finally, I would like to close this book with my story, which includes an account of the role contemplation has played in my own life.

BUSINESS

The model for business organizations is changing rapidly. Large corporations like IBM and GM are downsizing and decentralizing. The work of people like Stephen Covey, Tom Peters, and Peter Senge is having a profound effect on the way people in business approach their work. Peter Senge's work is particularly pertinent here. Senge (1990) describes five important features of what he calls "the learning organization." Senge argues that organizations must become learning organizations if they are to prosper or even survive in today's world. He suggests (1990) that there are five components to a learning organization:

1. Systems Thinking
2. Personal Mastery

3. Mental Models
4. Building Shared Vision
5. Team Learning

The second component is particularly relevant to this book. Senge claims

> personal mastery is the discipline of continually clarifying and deepening our personal vision, of focusing our energies, of developing patience, and of seeing reality objectively. As such, it is an essential cornerstone of the learning organization–the learning organization's spiritual foundation. . . . The roots of this discipline lie in both Eastern and Western spiritual traditions, and in secular traditions as well. . . . The discipline of personal mastery. . . starts with clarifying the things that really matter to us, of living our lives in the service of our highest aspirations. (pp. 7-8)

Personal mastery involves a balance between defining our highest aspirations and seeing things clearly. According to Senge: "*[for a person with a high level of mastery, such] a vision is a calling rather than simply a good idea.* They see 'current reality' as an ally, not an enemy" (p. 142). Senge also states that personal mastery is a process, a lifelong discipline. This idea is very similar to one of Covey's seven habits of highly effective people, beginning with the end in mind. This means taking the long-term view so that we assess everything against our life aspirations.

Senge characterizes people with high levels of personal mastery as having a sense of connectedness and compassion. They see the larger picture in a deeply integrative way. Senge (1990) quotes Einstein:

> [The human being] experiences himself, his thoughts and feelings as something separated from the rest–a kind of optical delusion of our consciousness. This delusion is a kind of prison for us, restricting us to our personal desires and to affection for a few persons nearest to us. Our task must be to free ourselves from this prison by widening our circle of compassion to embrace all living creatures and the whole of nature in its beauty. (p. 170)

Senge specifically refers to meditation and visualization as a means to personal mastery. Senge believes that meditation, in the form of contemplative prayer or simply quieting the mind, is a way to access our subconscious mind. which can be a source of creativity. Personal mastery allows the integration of reason and intuition. Senge (1990) also suggests that various spiritual disciplines let us see things more clearly:

> The power of the truth, seeing reality more and more as it is, cleansing the lens of perception, awakening from self-imposed distortions of reality–different expressions of a common principle in almost all the world's great philosophic and religious systems. Buddhists strive to achieve the state of "pure observation," of seeing reality directly. Hindus speak of "witnessing," observing themselves and their lives with an attitude of spiritual detachment. The Koran ends with the phrase, "What a tragedy that man must die before he wakes up." The power of the truth was no less central to early Christian thinking, although it has lost its place in Christian practice over the last two thousand years. (p. 161)

Stephen Covey (1990) has a similar message. For example, he encourages people to have private victories, which can involve personal mastery. He suggests that our outward success reflects our inward successes and our ability to witness and accept ourselves as well as to develop dominion over self. Covey has made reference to meditation and visualization as vehicles for developing the private victories. Covey cites religious leader David O. McKay, who said: "The greatest battles of life are fought out daily in the silent chambers of the soul" (cited in Covey, 1990, p. 294). Covey (1990) adds:

> If you win the battles there, if you settle the issues that inwardly conflict, you feel a sense of peace, a sense of knowing what you're about. And you'll find that the public victories–where you tend to think cooperatively, to promote the welfare and good of other people, and to be genuinely happy for other people's successes–will follow naturally. (p. 294)

In summary, both Senge and Covey argue that personal mastery is one of the essential components to a successful organizational life. When it is included, work takes on a sacred quality. Senge cites the example of a *Christian Science Monitor* reporter who, on visiting the Matushita Corporation, stated, "There is an almost religious atmosphere about the place, as if work itself were considered something sacred" (p. 145). I believe that this sense of the sacred arises from the flow experience, which occurs when we are deeply focused on what we are doing. In this highly attentive state, we enjoy what we are doing in a very unself-conscious manner. All of us have experienced this state, but somehow it rarely comes into our work. Often we feel disengaged from work, but through contemplation there is the opportunity to see every task in a new light. This light comes simply from our focused awareness. Through the media, television, and our fast-paced society, we have lost the ability to concentrate. Meditation, mindfulness, and other forms of contemplation allow us to reconnect with our work.

The CEO of Houghton Mifflin, Nader Darehshori, claims that he is more productive since he started meditating. At 5:30 P.M. he sits at his desk and focuses on his breathing for about 15 minutes. He has been so impressed with the effects of meditation on his own work that he introduced meditation to twelve Boston publishing company executives who usually work 12- to 14-hour days.

The head of Coors Beer, William Coors, has been meditating for years, and because of the positive effects in his own life, meditation training has been offered to his employees. He claims that meditation is the one factor that has helped lower the company's mental health costs 27 percent since 1987.

In calling for North American companies to be more productive, we have often taken the outside-in approach by motivating workers through either fear or rewards. Recent surveys, however, indicate that workers want work to be fulfilling. One way to encourage this search for fulfillment is to facilitate, but certainly not mandate, various forms of contemplation in the workplace. Through contemplation people could reconnect to their work in a deeper and more complete way.

SPORTS

Some of the best examples of the flow experience come from sports. Tim Gallwey (1978) has characterized this state of being as Self 2. Self 1, on the other hand, is that state of consciousness where we have a heightened sense of ourselves as separate. Self 1 is characterized by tension, boredom, insecurity, worry, confusion, and hesitation. In contrast, Self 2 arises when we feel free, light, flowing, relaxed, rhythmic, joyful, and exhilarated. We move into Self 2 when we are not so self-conscious and, instead, move more instinctively, trusting our body to do the right thing. Self 1 is often most common when we are beginning to learn a sport such as golf or skiing. After attaining some basic level of competence and confidence, we can begin to experience Self 2. George Sheehan (1978) gives a good description of Self 2 as experienced when he is running:

> In those miles downwind, I have a new vision of myself and the universe. The running is easy, automatic, yet full of power, strength, precision. A tremendous energy pours through my body. I am whole and holy. And the universe is whole and holy and full of meaning. In the passion of this running, truth is being carried, as the poet says, alive into my heart. (pp. 226-227)

Michael Murphy (1992) suggests that "athletic feats can mirror contemplative graces" (p. 444). Murphy states that "success is correlated with constant presence in the moment. Indeed, concentration can produce a state of mind graced by extraordinary clarity and focus" (p. 444). He (1992) cites the experiences of British golfer Tony Jacklin to support his claim:

> When I'm in this state, this cocoon of concentration, I'm fully in the present, not moving out of it. I'm aware of every half inch of my swing. . . . I'm absolutely engaged, involved in what I'm doing at that particular moment. (p. 444)

Many athletes have practiced meditation and visualization to create the conditions for the flow experience to arise. The memory of Arthur Ashe is still vivid in my mind, as he would meditate between sets on the tennis court. Jack Nicklaus (1974) uses visualization in the following way:

> I never hit a shot, not even in practice, without having a very sharp, in-focus picture of it in my head. It's like a color movie. First I "see" the ball where I want it to fin-

> ish, nice and white and sitting up high on the bright green grass. Then the scene quickly changes and I "see" the ball going there: its path, trajectory, and shape, even its behavior on landing. Then there is a fadeout, and the next scene shows me making the kind of swing that will turn the previous images into reality. (pp. 79-80)

Sports psychologist Richard Suinn discusses the type of visualization that is most effective.

> This imagery is more than visual. It is also tactile, auditory, emotional, and muscular. One swimmer reported that the scene in her mind changed from black and white to color as soon as she dove mentally into a pool, and she could feel the coldness of the water. A skier who qualified for the U.S. Alpine ski team experienced the same "irritability" that she felt during actual races when she mentally practiced being in the starting gate. Without fail, athletes feel their muscles in action as they rehearse their sport. (Cited in Murphy, 1992, p. 445)

Athletes, then, use both meditation and visualization to enhance their performance. Various forms of contemplative practice seem to make it more likely that the athlete will enter Jacklin's cocoon of deeply focused attention.

ARTISTS AND WRITERS

The flow experience is also central to the arts. The creative process is usually stifled by ego censorship, while it is enhanced by a state similar to Gallwey's Self 2, where we feel deeply connected to the process at hand. Writers and artists have meditated to enhance the flow of their writing or artistic performance. Arnold Schulman, for example, a noted screenwriter and playwright, has practiced Zen meditation for most of his adult life. He finds that he learned to concentrate more clearly on his work as a result of meditation. He is also able to write for longer periods, with only three or four hours of rest each day. (Carrington, 1977, p. 239)

Mary Caroline Richards, noted for her pottery and writing, suggests that contemplation and art are closely connected. Her form of contemplation is called centering. Centering is a process that involves opening outwards and then integrating experiences with the psyche. This process leads to what Richards calls the "artistic mind" (cited in Miller, 1988, p. 93). The process of stretching our consciousness, as Richards calls it, is a daily practice. The artistic mind is perhaps best described by Rilke, who said, "I live my life in growing orbits that stretch out over the things of the world. I am circling around the ancient tower. I have been circling for a thousand years and I don't know whether I am a hawk, a storm, or a great song" (cited in Miller, 1988, pp. 92-93). Art, for Richards, is a way of expressing our interior life as it allows us to bring our spirituality into form; she says, "In effect we pour our souls into the art through the materials we use, for example, paint, clay, dance, or music" (cited in Miller, 1988, p. 94). It is through her meditation, or centering, that Richards finds that she is more open to creative intuitions that spark her creativity, whether it is writing poetry or working with clay. Contemplation allows creativity to flow. For Richards, "creativity is the natural tendency. . . . Creativity is what we are" (cited in Miller, 1988, p. 95).

Another writer who practices meditation is Peter Matthiessen. Peter has written more than twenty books, including both fiction and nonfiction works. In a writer so prolific, various themes appear in his work, but perhaps the most prominent include (1) a deep respect for the natural world in books such as *The Wind Birds*, *Wildlife in America*, (2) a concern for social justice, as in *Sal Si Puedes*, *In the Spirit of Crazy Horse*, *Indian Country*, and *Men's Lives*, and (3) a concern with the inner life, as in *The Snow Leopard* and *Nine-Headed Dragon River: Zen Journals 1969-1982.*

In the 1960s Matthiessen began Zen meditation practice. His first wife, Deborah Love, introduced him to meditation. One of the most moving parts of *Nine-Headed Dragon River* is Peter's description of how the Zen students supported Deborah when she was dying of cancer in 1971. They came into the hospital room and acted as volunteer nurses. The head nurse at the hopital said she had never seen such support and love. She said to Peter, "I don't know what you Zen people do, but you're doing something right."

Also moving is Peter's description of his relationship to his guide, the Sherpa Tukten, in *The Snow Leopard*. Peter remarked that "Tukten is the kind of teacher one profoundly hopes for, all the more because he was not a guru and had no idea that he was my teacher at all. His teaching was manifested very simply in his day-to-day behavior" (Miller, 1988, p. 81). Peter felt a deep connection to Tukten, a bond he describes in *Nine-Headed Dragon River* as a "thread between us, like a black thread of live nerve." American Indians have also served him as teachers.

Zen has helped Peter live more in the present moment. He states that if we can develop this immediate and direct awareness of things as they are, if we are fully present when we take tea or wash dishes or go for a walk, we will inevitably preceive a more complete reality. Matthiessen has a small meditation hall on his property, and he is committed to regular practice. He feels that meditation has made him less judgmental and has directly affected his work in novels like *Far Tortuga*. Of course, the connection is very evident in his works dealing with spirituality, such as *Nine-Headed Dragon River*.

HEALTH

Perhaps there is no better example of how a person can integrate contemplative practice into daily life than Jon Kabat-Zinn. Jon is director of a Stress Reduction Program at the University of Massachusetts Medical Center in Worcester. He is author of *Full Catastrophe Living* (1990) and was recently interviewed by Bill Moyers for the *Healing and the Mind* series that appeared on PBS. The Stress Reduction Program began when patients with chronic pain were referred to Jon after all of the usual medical procedures had been followed. In a sense, the Stress Reduction Program was a last resort. Patients include individuals with serious illnesses such as cancer and heart disease as well as people having problems with headaches and high blood pressure. There are also some people who are experiencing anxiety and general discomfort, although the doctor cannot find anything specifically wrong. In general, these people have exhausted all the traditional approaches to relieving pain.

Kabat-Zinn believes that ultimately each person has resources within to deal with the problems that they are facing. Jon explains:

> Although we can influence healing in many ways, the ultimate capacity for healing lies within the person. In our program we challenge people so that they can help themselves get better. We introduce people to techniques such as meditation that are not traditionally associated with medicine but which have proven to be powerful tools for healing and personal transformation.

Through these methods we hope people discover their
ability to heal themselves. (Cited in Miller, 1988, p. 41)

Jon himself has been practicing various forms of Buddhist meditation as well as hatha yoga for many years. In the Stress Reduction
Program he introduces these techniques, but they are removed from
the Buddhist context. The people in the program come for an eight-
week course for two hours once a week. In the sixth week there is a
day-long session where people practice mindfulness meditation. For a
whole day they practice both sitting and walking meditation. Kabat-
Zinn comments on what many people experience:

One of the consequences of mindfulness meditation is a
profound sense of relaxation. Another consequence is
the falling away of personalized clinging and attach-
ment. People see into the deeper aspects of their being
and, of course, this can be very liberating. . . . Their
symptoms may not have been totally relieved, but they
usually gain something more important: self-under-
standing and acceptance, which are fundamental to any
healing. (Cited in Miller, 1988, p. 43)

There is research that supports Jon's work. In one study of 220
patients there was an average symptom reduction of 30 to 40 percent,
and for some patients there was a reduction in symptoms of 80 to 90
percent. These results were maintained as long as four years with some
of the patients. These data contrast with studies of traditional medical
pain reduction techniques, such as the use of cortisone, where on the
average there is no symptom loss.

Jon suggests that the difference in his program is that people learn
to tap their inner resources for healing rather than relying on external
treatments. He says: "People also learn that all pain will not go away
and so they learn how to accept pain in their life. . . . Through meditation they connect with their true nature and they find this experience
very liberating." People no longer see themselves as just a "liver
patient" or a "dialysis patient." They see into their true and less limited
identity. The program uses meditation as inquiry into the nature of
things and attention is essential to this process. For example, Jon
comments: "If someone is upset about making mortgage payments we
turn our attention to that instead of saying forget about it and relax.

By turning our attention to whatever we are concerned about lets us eventually develop wisdom" (cited in Miller, 1988, pp. 44-47).

Jon has even worked with physicians and lawyers. Jon stated:

> We have weekend retreats for physicians and health care workers that focus on the development of mindfulness. They come to the retreat expecting to get a lecture on stress and we ask them to sit quietly for an hour. This is often very difficult for doctors who are on the go all day. By sitting for an hour, they can learn more about pain than they ever learned before because they experience it directly in their own bodies. One doctor who had attended professional development courses for many years said that this was the first time he had an opportunity to work on himself, all the other seminars were about what he can do for the patient. (Cited in Miller, 1988, p. 47).

Meditation, then, allows the doctor to overcome the doctor-patient duality. Kabat-Zinn comments that meditation and medicine are similar in meaning. He states that the root meaning of the word medicine is not to cure but to measure. The idea here is that everything has its own internal measure and medicine helps restore the right internal measure. Meditation is also the measuring of body, mind, and thought, through attention. Meditation and medicine, then, are close to each other in their root meaning; both emphasize restoring the right internal measure.

In his work with court judges, Jon commented that the judges have to sit all day but have never had training in sitting. The judges are "supposed to demonstrate equanimity, compassion, and discriminating wisdom" and they have never had any systematic training in these areas (cited in Miller, 1988, p. 48).

Many of the people who attend the Stress Reduction Program continue with the meditation. Almost half are able to continue with some form of sitting practice, while close to 90 percent continue with mindfulness in daily life. One of the reasons people continue with the practice is that meditation and mindfulness let them be aware of their reaction to pain. Often the emotional baggage that a person carries around about a particular problem or illness contributes to the suffering. Meditative awareness allows the person to see how the mind's reaction contributes to the suffering and allows the individual to be less reactive to the pain. This in itself can be profoundly healing.

Jon believes that he has learned more from the people in his program than they learn from him. He says: "I am very moved when I hear people say how simply paying attention can be so healing" (cited in Miller, 1988, p. 37).

As mentioned earlier, Jon has been practicing Buddhist meditation for most of his adult life. Jon is married and has children, and he comments that children are the supreme Zen masters. He got the title for his book from Zorba the Greek, who talks about having a family as the full catastrophe, so what we are practicing as parents is "full catastrophe Zen" (cited in Miller, 1988, p. 40). Kabat-Zinn applies meditative awareness to every aspect of his life, so the work is keeping the vibrancy of the practice in the face of the catastrophe. Jon feels that he doesn't need any special place to do the practice.

As Jon mentioned, there are physicians who have chosen to do inner work. I interviewed two: Greg O'Connell and Don Woodside. Greg is an oncologist who works with women who have cancers of the cervix, uterus, and ovaries. Greg did not start his practice as an oncologist, but moved into this form of medical practice because it allows for longer and more meaningful contact with his patients. He didn't want to see the patient only just before and after an operation.

Greg was introduced to meditation in 1985. On the advice of a friend, he went to a meditation retreat at the Insight Meditation Society (IMS) conducted by Ruth Denison. He also joined a meditation group in his own community of Hamilton, Ontario, that meets once a week. In 1992 Greg went on another retreat in England. There he had a profound transformational experience. At this retreat he experienced a deep connection to all life that has lasted beyond the retreat. Greg finds it difficult to put the experience into words, but he feels the boundaries dissolving between himself and his environment. He feels intimately related to all that surrounds him, for example, the trees and the flowers. As Greg's sense of separateness has dissolved, he finds the experience very liberating and refreshing. He doesn't seem to get upset by the little things and doesn't feel the pressure to be the perfect physician or the best surgeon. When Greg walks from his office to the hospital, he finds that he becomes aware of his breath or his walking, and this renews his sense of connectedness. Greg feels more a part of the flow of life.

Greg has also had to deal with cancer in his own life. He has a rare form of cancer that affects the neck and head areas. One night before the physicians were going to do a procedure on the affected areas, Greg spent what he calls a night of terror. He lay awake all night, and after awhile he started to focus on his breathing. He believes that the meditation let him get through the experience. Greg says (1993): "I was very, very thankful that I had this vehicle." Because of his own experiences with cancer Greg is able to relate very directly and compassionately with his patients. He says that talking about his own experiences allows his patients to talk about their own fears and concerns.

Greg is also trying to organize a supportive care program that assists caregivers and patients. Greg would like to overcome some of the fragmentation that exists, so that there is continuous support for patients as they deal with cancer. He describes what the patients experience as a journey, and he feels that the health care system should provide compassionate support for that journey.

Through meditation and his experience with cancer, Greg O'Connell provides a unique form of health care to his cancer patients. At the center of his work is a deep sense of connection to his patients and the flow of life.

Don Woodside is part of the same meditation group that Greg attends once a week in Hamilton, Ontario. Don is a psychiatrist who works mostly with severely disturbed adolescents. The day I interviewed Don, he had been working with a girl who was severely depressed and was also suicidal.

Don has been meditating for many years. He was introduced to meditation in the late sixties when he was in Asia, and then came back to meditative practice in the early eighties when he started attending retreats at IMS. He has attended many retreats, some of them as long as three months. Besides Buddhist meditation, Don has also practiced contemplative exercises developed by St. Ignatius. A very important part of Don's life is attending Quaker meetings every week. I asked Don if he had a special teacher, and he answered that the Buddha and Christ were his teachers.

Don (1993) suggests that meditation has helped him become more calm and compassionate. He says, "I am much less defensive." He acknowledges that he is more in touch with his emotions and that he "can express himself from the heart." He feels a much deeper appreciation of life and death. He comments that meditation has been described as learning how to die, and he feels that meditation has helped him come to terms with his own mortality. Don (1993) states:

> Everything is so precious . . . the light in the sky, the
> trees, the leaves and the colors. I can really just appre-
> ciate all this as whole at any one time. It doesn't mean
> that I am free from anxieties about my future, but I can
> set things in a larger perspective.

For a psychiatrist working with troubled people, the qualities of
calmness and compassion are very important. Don believes that coun-
seling techniques are also essential to his practice, but meditation
allows him to access his intuition so he knows what technique is
appropriate at a given moment. He also finds that he doesn't react as
emotionally to certain situations; in other words, he doesn't get caught
in the patient's melodrama. This perspective is also helpful in working
with other health care workers, because it helps prevent egos from
taking over.

Because Don works with severely disturbed patients, he does not
employ meditation directly with his clients. However, he is very interested in the connection between psychotherapy and meditation.
Although there are certainly differences, Don notes that both psychotherapy and meditation ask the person to be mindful and to watch
for patterns and connections.

SLOWING DOWN

The second part of this chapter outlines ways in which we can
begin to live the contemplative life. The contemplative life is ultimately
a life of purpose, joy, and compassion. It allows us to examine what is
really important in life so that we are not pulled into pointless activity
that tends to fragment and deaden our being.

Slowing Down

Our lives can be frantic. At times we may feel that events have
taken over, as the pace of life seems to quicken with each passing year.
We find that a typical day can go something like the following:

We awaken each morning and often one of the first things that we
do is turn on the radio or television to find out whether the world made
it through last night without a major catastrophe. Mornings can be
very rushed as we get dressed, make breakfast, and help our children

also get ready for the day. We often leave the house in the morning feeling already somewhat frazzled. As we commute to work, the drive can get our adrenalin pumping faster, for the snarl of traffic can sometimes be overwhelming. As we arrive at work, we are often confronted with a long list of activities for the day, which may involve meetings and encounters with others that are stressful. At the end of the day, we may again face the problems of commuting, as well as errands on the way home. When we arrive home, there can be demands of family as well as the work of preparing and/or cleaning up the evening meal. The evenings are sometimes filled with meetings or work that we have brought home. At the end of the day, we may feel exhausted. Although the weekends are supposed to be for relaxation, they are often just as programmed as the weekday, with jobs around the house, shopping, and social activities.

My students, in their meditation journals, often report on "the list" of things they have to do. Often this list can be quite long. Through contemplation, however, we begin to see things on the list that we don't have to do. From a contemplative approach, we can begin to slow down. We start to do just one thing at a time rather than trying to do several activities at once. We can also build little gaps in the day. If we are driving or walking from one place to another, we can give ourselves extra time so that we can enjoy the drive or walk, just as Greg O'Connell enjoys the walk from his office to the hospital. By slowing down the pace of lives, we feel less controlled by external events and we can find a new source of energy.

Slowing down does not mean becoming a zombie. It involves performing more daily activities with a freshness and focus. Mindfulness aids the whole process of slowing down by helping us bring attention to our daily tasks.

Meditation/Mindfulness

I have already discussed various approaches to meditation in chapter 2. Here I want to say that meditation should not be limited to the time that we are sitting. The freshness of mind and awareness that arises during sitting practice we can bring into every aspect of our lives. As Shinzen Young says, after we have meditated for a while, we find that our lives become filled with peace, presence, and focus. We gradually bring this presence into our work and our relationships with others. Our activity takes on a more sacred quality with this awareness.

We find that we don't want anything from anybody, and thus we are free to relate to others in a more open and direct way. There are no hidden agendas in our relationships.

Through meditation and mindfulness, we become, in Zen master Dogen's words, "enlightened by everything in the world" (cited in Winokur, p. 66). This means an intimacy with the trees, the flowers, the grass, the animals, and the people that surround us. Through meditation we find that the universe and the earth are our friends; we are comfortable with life.

Acceptance of Ambiguity and Imperfection

We live in a society where events are "managed." For years our businesses and education systems were run according to management by objective (MBO). The MBO approach allowed for little ambiguity. However, MBO didn't work very well. The Japanese began to clobber American business, and we found that their approach to management was not based on MBO. Instead, there was a much greater acceptance of the unpredictable. Pascale and Athos (1981) state:

> Ambiguity, uncertainty, and imperfection, with their many shades of meaning, carry different connotations in the East than in the West. In the United States, for example, when a situation is "ambiguous," the implication is that it is incomplete, unstable, and needs clearing up. In Japan, in contrast, ambiguity is seen as having both desirable and undesirable aspects. The Japanese often seek a great deal of predictable order. But in other respects, having to do with many organizational matters, they are also willing to flow with things. More ambiguity, uncertainty, and imperfection in organizations is acceptable to them than to us as an immutable fact of life, what philosophers in the West have called "existential givens." By this they mean that such conditions just *are,* and, accordingly, the sooner we accept that they exist the better things will go. Regarding them as *enemies* gets our adrenalin pumping for a hopeless battle. Regarding them as conditions to be reduced or lived with, as appropriate to the situation, makes more sense. (p. 141)

One area where we seem to have little tolerance for ambiguity is the expectations or models we hold about other people. We seem to carry a model in a our head for how other people should behave. We become easily irritated by how other people dress, speak, or walk. As Ram Dass has noted, when we go into nature, we don't carry a model of how a tree or a flower should be. We generally accept and even delight in the diversity of nature. Yet with people, the least variation from our norms can make us frustrated and irritated. Ultimately, we need to let go of the models we hold for other people. Of course, we have expectations for people in our classrooms and the workplace, but I am not referring to these expectations. Instead, we often find ourselves becoming upset over superficial aspects of people's behavior that we have no right to control. Much of contemplative practice is learning to simply let go, and letting go of our models of how others should behave can do much to let us feel free and at peace.

Creating Gaps

In our world we seem almost compulsive in filling up the day so that there is very little free time. We can find our days so filled that there is little time to simply relate directly to what is happening. In short, we have little respect for the gaps or intervals in our lives. In contrast, the Japanese as well as those of other cultures accept the pauses and gaps. The Japanese, for example, call this space, or interval, *ma*.

> Respect for *ma* deters us from plunging ahead when the right time for action is still impending. Gifted actors and comedians, great speakers and leaders, have an instinct for this quality. We have all noted the *pause* just prior to an important point when participants are momentarily waiting for release from tension created in part by the pause itself. But, as in theater, so also in organizational life, the magic fusion between anticipation and execution often fizzles. We have all witnessed a flow of organizational events building effectively toward closure only to see the overeager clumsily destroy consensus with a premature plunge toward the finish line. Such haste is as disastrous in organizations as in the theater. (Pascale & Athos, 1981, p. 144)

We can also see the respect for space in Japanese paintings, for the drawing is usually placed within a large amount of space. The painting is not cluttered with too much detail, and the space allows us to appreciate the figures more.

Western culture is not comfortable with space or silence. For example, our homes tend to be filled with furniture and objects. We also find ourselves filling up silent moments with conversation, the radio, or television. I understand that in some indigenous cultures an individual can enter another person's abode, stay there for a while without saying anything, and then get up and leave. We know that if someone in our culture did this we would call for the white coats.

From a contemplative perspective, we can see and appreciate the balance between silence and sound, between space and figure. We learn how each is essential to the other rather than having sound and material objects dominate our lives. The contemplative approach brings a balance into our lives.

Witnessing

Another vehicle for creating more space and slowing down is the witness. The witness is that place in our consciousness that compassionately sees everything from a nonjudgmental perspective. The witness sees the suffering and joy from a compassionate perspective. It looks at the inner "tapes" that can take over our lives. These are the tapes of addiction, compulsion, and other repeated patterns. From the perspective of the witness, we can begin to see these patterns more clearly and find that we do not immediately get caught up in the tape.

For example, the witness can watch the patterns between ourselves and others. If I find myself getting locked in arguments with my wife or child, the compassionate witness can provide a place where I can see what is happening. This perspective allows me to step aside and not be so reactive to everything that happens. I am not immediately drawn into the conflict. Gradually, we may find that the pattern begins to loosen its hold. Yes, it still may remain in some form, but the compulsion and rigidity associated with the pattern are significantly diminished.

Nutrition and Exercise

We cannot ignore our bodies. Like everything else in our life the body needs to be honored and respected. Through contemplation we gradually witness the foods that make us feel well and those foods that bring a sense of heaviness. Gradually, our diets may change to food and drink that is lighter. We may eat less red meat and cut back on the fat in our diet. This change in diet simply comes from seeing connections between food and how we feel. It doesn't come from reading about what we "should" eat. In general, changes that result from a contemplative approach tend to be natural ones that arise from our awareness.

We may learn that we feel better if we exercise. The exercise does not have to be strenuous. Walking will do. Dean Ornish (1990) has found that meditation, a healthy diet, and exercise actually reverse the direction of heart disease. He has provided some striking evidence of how rather simple changes in our lifestyle can have profound effects on our health.

It is important that we not be compulsive about our food or diet. We don't have to be rigid or obsessive about any of the things I am suggesting as part of the slowing down process. The contemplative approach to life involves a loosening up, not a tightening up. It is important that the contemplative approach not become a dogma or set of rules that promotes disconnection.

Humor

Humor helps us lighten up rather than tighten up. It is a wonderful source of healing and joy. I am speaking of humor that allows us to laugh at ourselves and with others rather than the forms of humor that exploit or categorize. We have evidence from people like Norman Cousins and Raymond Moody that laughter is good for us. The story of Norman Cousins is well known. When he heard he had a terminal illness, he took vitamin C and then started watching Marx Brothers films in his hospital room. He gradually got well through this therapy.

Chesterton said: "Angels can fly because they take themselves lightly" (cited in Winokur, 1990, p. 38). Humor helps in this process, as it loosens the hold of the ego. It is so easy for us to get caught in our personal melodramas. Divorce, problems at work, or difficulties with our children can fill our minds with worry. It is helpful, then, to see our lives as a part of the *lila*, the dance or rhythm of life, rather than separating ourselves off with our own problems.

Stephen Nachmanovitch (1990) describes the meaning of *lila:*

> There is an old Sanskrit word, *lila*, which means play. Richer than our word, it means divine play, the play of creation, destruction, and recreation, the folding and unfolding of the cosmos. *Lila*, free and deep, is both the delight and enjoyment of this moment, and the play of God. It also means love.
>
> *Lila* may be the simplest thing there is–spontaneous, childish, disarming. But as we grow and experience the complexities of life, it may also be the most difficult and hard-won achievement imaginable, and its coming to fruition is a kind of homecoming to our true selves. (p. 1)

To approach life with a sense of *lila* can allow us to reawaken to the basic joy of life and provide a broader perspective from which to view our lives.

Art

Music and art can help our souls sing. Listening to music is particularly therapeutic. Like so many others, I find the music of Mozart very healing. I would like to quote Jacques Lusseyran (1987) about the effects of music on his own being:

> The world of violins and flutes, of horns and cellos, of fugues, scherzos and gavottes, obeyed laws which were so beautiful and so clear that all music seemed to speak of God. My body was not listening, it was praying. My spirit no longer had bounds, and if tears came to my eyes, I did not feel them running down because they were outside me. I wept with gratitude every time the orchestra began to sing. (p. 93)
>
> I loved Mozart so much, I loved Beethoven so much that in the end they made me what I am. They molded my emotions and guided my thoughts. Is there anything in me which I did not, one day, receive from them? I doubt it. (pp. 92-93)

We need to sing more. The soul loves a good song, and when we sing the song, our souls rejoice. Jack Kornfield (1993) tells a wonderful story about how a tribe in Africa connects each child with a song. When the mother wants to conceive a child with her mate she goes and sits under a tree until she can hear the song of the child she hopes to conceive. Once she hears the song she comes back to the village and shares it with her husband. They sing the song while they make love, hoping the child hears them. When the baby starts to grow in the womb, the mother, along with other women in the village, sings the song to it. Throughout labor and during birth the baby is greeted by his or her song. Most of the village learns the song so that it can be sung to the child whenever he or she becomes hurt or is in danger. The song is also sung during various rituals in the child's life. For example, the song is sung when the child marries. When the person is on the deathbed, friends and relatives gather to sing the song for the last time.

MY STORY

In education, as in other areas, there is a lot of emphasis on story. People are being encouraged to tell their stories as a way of interpreting or framing their own experiences. In my classes at OISE, I tell my own story. I find that students welcome hearing a teacher's journey.

I was born in 1943 and raised in Kansas City, Missouri, where my parents provided a loving and secure environment. My mother's name, Joy, was very appropriate, as she had a wonderful sense of humor. She could make me and others in her life laugh. I can remember many times in my childhood sharing a smile, giggle, or laugh. My father, who seemed remote in my childhood, became a more important figure in my life during adolescence and young adulthood. We both liked sports, and we would talk a lot about baseball and particularly football at the University of Missouri, where both my mother and father went to school. My father respected my right to make my own decisions, even though some of my decisions were not those that he would have made. My grandmother was the other significant adult in my life. She introduced me to the wonder of music by giving me a recording of Beethoven's Fifth Symphony when I was in Grade 6, and to this day I have found a spiritual connection in music, particularly the work of Mozart and Haydn. My grandmother also introduced me to Tolstoy's spiritual writing when I was in high school. I had good friends growing up, but I also remember spending a lot of time by myself, as I particularly liked to read.

I have an older brother, Bill, and over the years we have grown closer. He now lives in Texas, but we get together at least once a year, usually at a Missouri football game.

I attended the University of Missouri for my B.A. and then went to Harvard in 1965 to pursue a Master of Arts in Teaching. It was in Boston that I met my first wife, Jean, whom I married in December 1967. Jean came from an Boston Irish background that was so different from my midwestern background, yet it was clear from the beginning that we were meant to be together.

Jean and I began our married life in the Midwest, as I worked at Grinnell College and the University of Missouri at Kansas City (UMKC). Our first year of marriage was that turbulent year of 1968. Like so many Americans, I still remember vividly where we were when Martin Luther King and Bobby Kennedy were shot. I also recall that August, when we were moving to Kansas City, where I would begin a job teaching at the University of Missouri at Kansas City. The Russians had invaded Czechoslovakia, and when we were settling in our new apartment in Kansas City, we watched the riots at the Democratic National Convention in Chicago on television. The debates between Gore Vidal and William Buckley, I felt, characterized the deep divisions of that time.

That year of 1968, I began my spiritual search. I had been raised a Christian (Disciples of Christ), but as I confronted the draft and the Vietnam War, I needed something more to deal with the anxiety I was feeling. I had filed a CO (conscientious objector) statement that was not pacifist, but directed against U.S. intervention in Vietnam. Thoreau and Emerson have always been important teachers for me and I quoted Thoreau (1967) in my statement:

It is not a man's duty, as a matter of course, to devote himself to the eradication of any, even the most enormous wrong; he may still properly have other concerns to engage him; but it is his duty, at least, to wash his hands of it. . . . If the injustice is part of the necessary friction to the machine of government, let it go . . . but if it is of such a nature that it requires you to be the agent of injustice to another, then, I say, break the law. (pp. 146, 148)

Since I believed that the U.S. intervention was wrong, I was pre-
pared to resist the draft and thus break the law. Jean and I had decided
that if I was inducted we would go to Canada. The possibility of such a
change in my life created a tremendous amount of stress. I suffered
from dizzy spells and nervous tension. The stress began to interfere
with my work at UMKC, so I began to look for ways to deal with my
problems. I tried hypnosis, but it didn't help. Sometime during the fall,
I read Jess Stearn's *Yoga, Youth and Reincarnation*, which described
some simple hatha yoga exercises, and I began to practice them every
day. Within weeks I began to feel more relaxed. In short, the draft
started me on my spiritual journey. I became interested in the spiritual
framework that underpinned the yoga and began reading about
Eastern spiritual practices.

I received my induction notice in April of 1969, and Jean and I
began to make our plans to go to Canada. We emigrated to Toronto in
June of that year, and I began my doctoral studies in education at the
Ontario Institute for Studies in Education and the University of
Toronto. The pain of leaving my parents that June morning in 1969 is
still vivid in my memory. I can recall them standing sadly at the door
as Jean and I drove away in the car. When we arrived in Toronto the
next day, we found that our furniture hadn't arrived at our apartment,
so Jean and I bought air mattresses and army blankets so we could
sleep in our frigid apartment. That summer I alternated between exhil-
aration and depression, as I felt at home in Canada, yet I often became
depressed at the thought that I might never again be able to travel to
the United States to see my family. In a sense, going to Canada was
like a death, because I had to let go of so much.

Eventually, we settled into life in Toronto. Our first child, Patrick,
was born there in 1970. When I graduated, I took a job in Thunder
Bay, Ontario, working with the Ontario Institute for Studies in
Education in their field office. My work involved working with schools
in a consultant's capacity. Thunder Bay is located 200 miles north of
Duluth, Minnesota, and is relatively isolated. Snow settles on the
ground in November and doesn't leave until the beginning of April.

Helping me through these difficult years of change was my wife,
Jean. Her warmth and love provided the support that carried me
through these transitions. We both began to see our marriage as a
spiritual partnership or an environment for our mutual spiritual
growth. Jean also did the hatha yoga, and we both shared an interest in
Eastern spirituality. The teachings of Ram Dass were helpful to us, and
I can still remember us falling asleep at night listening to his words on

tape. We both began to see that our lives had a meaning and purpose and that we were connected to something much larger than ourselves. It was through the Ram Dass literature that I was introduced to the work of Goldstein and Kornfield. In 1974 I ordered a set of tapes by Joseph Goldstein on meditation instruction. These tapes guided the beginning of a meditation practice that I have continued to this day.

In 1976 Jean's father died, and in 1977 my mother passed away. The teachings of Kubler-Ross, Goldstein, and Ram Dass were very helpful to Jean and I and gave us a framework for understanding and working with the pain of these losses. They helped us see death as another transition rather than as the end. At the same time joy came with the birth of our daughter, Nancy, in 1976.

The year 1982 was another watershed year for Jean and I. I attended my first meditation retreat at Barre, Massachusetts, which was conducted by Jack Kornfield and Sharon Salzburg. The retreat was two weeks long and consisted of alternating sitting and walking meditations throughout the day. Much of the retreat was spent sitting in pain, as my knees and legs ached. However, halfway through the retreat I felt a sense of joy and rapture that permeated my whole being. Another crucial event in the retreat was that I saw a silhouette of Christ with his arms reaching out. What an irony! I had come to a Buddhist retreat and encountered the Christ spirit. Since that event I have been particularly drawn to spiritual teachers such as Thomas Merton who have explored the connection between Christianity and Buddhism. I have also studied "A Course in Miracles" and found it very helpful to my spiritual practice. Christ as a living presence is an important part of my spiritual practice.

Shortly after Christmas that year Jean told me she had a lump in her breast. I couldn't believe that she might have cancer. I remember that time as one in which she went for tests and I read as much as possible about the disease. We got a call one Sunday morning in January to say that she should come in that day for her surgery, which would take place the next day. Oh, how low I felt as I drove her to the hospital. After the operation, she lay in the room and I sat with her as I waited for her to awaken. As I looked at her, I felt such compassion, and I realized that we were connected beyond time and space. Until this point we had had a wonderful marriage based on love and trust, but now we started on a journey that resulted in spiritual union.

She recovered rapidly from the surgery, and her usual buoyant spirits returned. I remember her swinging her arm around two days after the surgery to show me how good she felt. The prognosis, however, wasn't good, since the cancer had spread to the lymph nodes. She had to have chemotherapy, and the treatments became increasingly more difficult. She lost her hair and was nauseated after each treatment. However, at the end of the treatments, she bounced back. The work of Bernie Siegel was very helpful to Jean as she began her fight with cancer.

At this time we moved to southern Ontario, where Jean loved her new home and surroundings. She reached out to make new friends and completed her honors degree in psychology. There was no evidence of any recurrence of the cancer for almost three years.

In September of 1986, however, we began our final journey together. I knew something was wrong when she had trouble remembering simple words. One morning I was going out shopping, and she couldn't remember the word "muffin." I cried out to her, "What's happening?" In a couple of weeks her memory got worse, and we rushed to the doctor's. He ordered an emergency CAT scan. We learned in a few days that the cancer had spread to the brain and that Jean had to undergo radiation treatment for two weeks. For several weeks, Jean could hardly express herself, and I had to be with her constantly. However, worse was to come, as she became very weak from the treatments; she lay sleeping on the couch except to get up for meals. She slept almost around the clock for six weeks; her legs became very thin. Around Christmas, she began to recover; she gained energy and her memory improved. In January it looked like she might fully recover, when we received more devastating news: the cancer had spread to her lung. She now began a new round of chemotherapy treatments. She handled these treatments very well and began to return to a normal lifestyle. The cancer was in remission. We were able to travel to Florida in March of 1987, and she was horseback riding in late April. People marveled at her spirits and how she recovered. Jean had hardly been able to walk in December, and in April she was living a normal life and horseback riding even while she was still taking the chemotherapy treatments.

The real miracle, however, was that there was a spiritual awakening that paralleled her awakening from her long rest in November and December. The last year of her life, Jean lived in Christ consciousness. Despite the pain and fear, her eyes radiated a warmth and glow that came from her spiritual heart. She was totally centered in a way that she had never been until she became sick. I remember her saying so often, even in the midst of dealing with her cancer, "I feel so blessed." Throughout our marriage Jean said that I was her teacher, but in the last year of her life, she became my teacher. I marveled at her courage and spiritual presence. The cancer made me surrender completely to what was happening. Through this whole experience, meditation provided a tremendous support. Since meditation allows us to accept pain in our own bodies, we are less fearful of being in the presence of others who are experiencing pain.

We got more bad news that fall, when we learned that the cancer had spread to the liver. She was treated again with chemotherapy. Again, she seemed to sail through the treatments, and we spent a wonderful Christmas together that year. We went to Florida with the kids in March, and as Jean walked the beach, she remarked, "This is heaven." She always loved the ocean, and was most joyful and peaceful when she was near the water. I couldn't have dreamed then that she would die in a few weeks. Jean's approach to life at that time was like the Zen story of the man who was hanging from a cliff facing certain death below when his grip finally tired. Despite the presence of death, the man reached out to take a strawberry growing on the cliffside and savored each mouthful as he ate it. Jean, who knew that she was going to die, savored each moment with her family whom she loved so deeply.

On April 11, 1988, Jean died at home where she wanted to be. She needed only Tylenol those last days. Despite the cancer she always felt blessed because of her family and the love that they returned to her. A few minutes after Jean died, my son Patrick came into the room and hugged his mother. I sat with Jean that evening and waited for the doctor to come to pronounce her dead. From one of Stephen Levine's books I read passages that help a soul move into the light. When the undertaker came, Nancy and Patrick picked out an outfit for their mother. I was amazed at the strength and calmness they showed in the presence of death.

It was through Jean that I learned about the fundamentals of life—suffering, love, and death. It was through this experience that the teachings of Buddha and Christ came alive. However, in the end it was clear that my wife, Jean, had become my most powerful and wisest teacher. By seeing our marriage as a spiritual partnership in which we helped each other through our respective crises, we could touch the oneness, the living spirit.

Gary Zukov, in his book *The Seat of the Soul*, suggests that before we incarnate we enter into a sacred contract with the universe about our work on earth. It is clear to me that Jean and I may have entered into an agreement to help each other come into the oneness. Zukov also suggests that when we fulfill our contract, we feel empowered. As I write this, it has been five years since Jean died. I have grieved. My heart has ached. Despite the pain, however, I feel empowered and whole. I feel the entire experience has given me strength and a deeper connection to life.

In 1991 I married Susan Drake, and thus have begun another journey. I continue to learn so much from each relationship in my life. It is important that I do not hold models from from my first marriage, so that this relationship can unfold in its own wonderful and mysterious way. Meditation and mindfulness continue to provide a ground for approaching each moment of life in my new relationship.

This year I turned 50. The contemplative approach lets us see life as blessed, in much the same way William Yeats saw it when he was fifty. He sat in a London coffee shop and suddenly felt overcome with happiness and gratitude: "That I was blessed—and could bless."

REFERENCES

Carrington, p. (1977). *Freedom in Meditation*. Garden City, NY: Anchor.

Covey, Stephen R. (1990). *The 7 habits of highly effective people*. New York: Simon & Schuster.

Doust, D. (1973, November 4). Opening the mystical door of perception in sport. *Sunday London Times*. November 4

Gallwey, T. and Kriegel, B. (January, 1978). "Inner skiing: Tame the mind, trust the body. *New Age*, pp. 46-51, 66-69.

Kabat-Zinn, Jon. (1990). *Full catastrophe living*. New York: Delacorte Press.

Kornfield, J. (1993). *A path with heart*. New York. Bantam.

Lusseyran, Jacques. (1987). *And there was light*. New York: Parabola.

Miller, John. (1981). *The compassionate teacher*. Englewood Cliffs, NJ: Prentice Hall.

——. (1988). Spiritual pilgrims. Unpublished manuscript.

Murphy, Michael. (1992). *The future of the body: Explorations into the further evolution of human nature*. New York: Jeremy p. Tarcher/Putnam.

Nachmanovitch, Stephen. (1990). *Free play*. Los Angeles: Jeremy p. Tarcher.

Nicklaus, J. (1974). *Golf my way*. New York: Simon & Schuster.

O'Connell, G. (1993). Personal interview with author.

Ornish, D. (1990). *Dr. Dean Ornish's program for reversing heart disease*. New York: Random House.

Pascale, R. T. & Athos, A. G. (1981). *The art of Japanese management*. New York: Warner.

Senge, Peter M. (1990). *The fifth discipline*. New York: Doubleday.

Sheehan, G. (1978). *Running and being*. New York: Warner Books

Thoreau, H. D. (1967). Civil disobedience. In p. Mayer (ed.), *The pacifist conscience*, Chicago: Gateway Editor, Henry Rigney.

Winokur, J. (Ed.) (1990). *Zen to go*. New York: Penguin.

Woodside, D. (1993). Personal interview with author.

Index

acceptance, 56
action meditation, 59
age of Gandhi, 108
Ahimsa, 105
akido, 58
Alara Kalama, 88
Alcott, Bronson, 98
Allah, 3, 65
Allen, Gay Wilson, 96, 100
analysis and reflection, vii
analytic philosophy, 17
analytic-synthetic dichotomy, 19
appropriate relationship, 9, 10
Aquinas, Thomas, 26
archetypes, 43
art, 155
asanas, 71, 72-81
asceticism, 88
Ashe, Arthur, 137
Ashkenazy, 21
Athos, A. G., 149, 150
Atman, 6, 24, 121
attention, 38
Autobiography, 93
awakened heart, 28

back stretch position, 76
balance, 10
basic science component, 18
Beatrice, 38, 39

Bernstein, R. J., 18
Beethoven, 8
being, 24, 25
being, not doing, 55
Benson, Herbert, 53, 120
Berne, P. H., 70, 71
Berry, Thomas, 13
Bhavagad Gita, 104,108
big mind, 61
big mind, long-enduring mind, 56
big story, 28
Black Act, 105
Black Elk, 33
Blake, William, 38, 40, 42
Bly, 10
Bodhi tree, 88
bodhisatva, 89
Bodian, S., 3
Bohm, David, 3, 33, 34, 44-45, 47
    implicate order, 41
Bonaventure, 23
bow position, 75
Boyer, Ernest, 119
Brahman, 3
bread of angels, 39
Buber, Martin, 25
    I-thou experience, 25
Buchman, M., 26
Buddha, viii, 29, 30, 57, 58, 87-91,
    115 159

Buddha-Nature, 6, 24, 121
Buddhism, 24, 65, 113
Buddhist retreat, 157

call to adventure, 29
Cambridge, 109
Campbell, Joseph, 28, 29, 89
Capaldi, N., 37
Capra, Fritjof, 100
Carmelite convents, 93
Carrington, Patricia, 3, 53, 66, 140
Catherine of Siena, 95
centering, 140
Chang, Garma C. C., 90
Channa, 88
Chesterton, G.K., 152
Christ, 57, 88, 157, 159
Christian and Buddhist forms of
    contemplation, 109
Christianity, 3, 24
    and Buddhism, 157
civil disobedience, 105
Clark, R. W., 133
cobra position, 72
cogitatio, 23
cognitive psychology, 11
collective unconscious, 3, 33, 43
Columbia, 108
communion, 114
compassionate attention, 2
compassionate time, 114
concentrated practice, 3
concentration on poetry or sacred
    texts, 122
Confessions (St. Augustine), 92
Connelly, F., 21
conscious love, 39
consciousness, 10, 45
contemplate and concentrate, 90
contemplatio, 23
contemplation applied to other
    fields, 135
    equated with concentration,
    110
    in the workplace, 138
    cosmological foundations, 30
contemplative life, 147
contemplative prayer, 92

contemplative practitioner, 17, 22,
    26
contemplative traditions, 115
contemplatives, 101
continuing vision, 40
Conway, Moncure, 97, 101
Coors, William, 138
cosmologies, indigenous peoples,
    33
Course in Miracles, A, 157
Cousins, Norman, 152
Covey, Stephen, 135, 137
    seven habits of highly effective
    people, 136
Crazy Horse, 33, 46
creating gaps, 150
Csikszentmihalyi, vii, 2, 5
culture of technology, 119

Dante, 29, 38-39, 41, 48
Darehshori, Nader, CEO of
    Houghton Mifflin, 138
de Chardin, Teilhard, 25
de Nicolas, Antonio T., 36, 38, 119,
    120
    Habits of Mind, 119
de Osuna, Francisco, 92
decentralized, 12
deep listening, 53
Denison, Ruth, 147
Deshimaru, T., 27
Desire, 30
detachment, 94
Dewey, John, 96
Dionysius, 37
direct awareness, 27
disconnection, 51
discrete degree, 40
distractedness, beginning stage, 93
Divine Comedy, The, 38, 39
Dogen, 149
Drake, Susan, 160
dreamtime, 45
dualistic view of reality, vii

Easwaran, Eknath, 65, 66, 103, 104,
    105, 106, 108
eclectic, 98

economy/environment, 10
ecstatic contemplative states, 93
ecstatic intimacy, 101
ego-based teaching, 122
ego-chatter, 27
eightfold path, 89, 90
Einstein, Albert, 33, 42, 131, 134
Eisenberg, John, 12
emergent qualities, 9
Emerson, Ralph Waldo, viii, 22, 25,
    41-42, 47, 48, 87, 96-103, 115
    householder, 101
    Philosopher of Democracy, 96
emotional forms of meditation, 58
empiricism, 98
engineering component, 18
enlightenment, 89
environment, 11
environmental crisis, 12
Erdman, J., 19
external stimuli, 1
eye of the flesh, reason,
    contemplation, 22, 23

Feinstein, D., 43
final stage–union with God, 94
find their lives, 46
first level of intuition, 24
Fischer, Louis, 107
Fish pose, 79
flat-line organization, 12
Flinders, Carol Lee, 92, 93, 94
flow experience, vii, 2
    from sports, 136
    in the arts, 140
following one's bliss, 28
four noble truths, 89
four waters, 93
fragmentation, 47
Frankl, Viktor, 71
Freedman, S. G., 25
Full Catastrophe Living, 5, 142
full catastrophe, 145
full catastrophe Zen, 145
Fullan, M., 21
Fuller, Margaret, 98
fundamental unity, 98
Furlong, M., 112, 113

Gallwey, Tim, 138
Gandhi, Karamchand, 103
Gandhi, Kasturbai, 103, 104, 108
Gandhi, Mahattma, viii, 65, 87, 95,
    96, 103-108, 116
    Salt March, 106-107
Gethsemani, 111, 113
Gita, 104
global village, 13
globalism, 14
God–the heavenly aura, 41
God, 3, 39, 57
Goethe, 98
Goldstein, Joseph, viii, 61, 62, 159
Gore, Al, 6
Gould, Stephen Jay, 5
grace, 57
Great Being, 30
great mother archetype, 43
Greenwood, D., 18
Griffin, Robert, 121
ground of being, 22
gurus and mysticism, 51

Habits of Mind, 119
half lotus position, 81
half twist position, 80
Hanh, Thich Nhat, 63, 64
Harijans, 105, 106
harmonious transpersonal system, 2
Harvard Divinity School, 97
hatha yoga, 58, 71
Hawaiian kahunas, 45
Hawthorne, Nathaniel, 101
Haydn, 8
head-knee pose, 76
hermitage, 113
hero archetype, 43
hierarchy/network, 10
higher education, 119
highest level of intuition, 24
Hindu, 58
Hindu mantras, 65
Hinduism, 3, 24
Holistic Curriculum, The, 122, 123
holistic education, 8, 122
holistic perspective, 6
holistic view, 22

Holmes Group, 21
Holmes, Oliver Wendell, 96, 102
hologram, 44
Holographic Universe, The, 45
holographic paradigm, 40
honesty, 38
Horowitz, 21
Hugh of St. Victor, 23
Hughes, Diana, 84
Huichol Indians, 46
humans and nature, connection
     between, 100
Hume, 98
humility, 94
humor, 152

I-thou experience (Buber), 25
idealism, 45
ideas or eternal forms (Plato), 37
implicate and explicate orders, 44
implicate order, 3, 33, 41
IMS (Insight Meditation Society),
     145, 146,
Incarnation order, 92
independent/interdependent, 9
Indian Congress Party, 106
individual–not an island, 11
infinitude, 99
inner self, 24
Inquisition, 93
Insight Meditation Society (IMS),
     145, 146
insight meditation (vipassana), 3,
     60-62, 122
instrumentalism, 13
integration of reason and intuition,
     135
intellectual approaches to
     meditation, 57-58
interconnectedness, 7
interdependence, 27
Interior Castle, The, 95
introspection, 7
intuition 24, 99
intuition and reflection, viii
intuitive response, 1
invisible world, 33
Islam, 3

Jacklin, Tony, 139
Jesus, 29, 35, 58, 60
Jesus prayer, 65
Judaism, 65
Jung, Carl, 3, 24, 33, 43-44, 54

Kabat-Zinn, Jon, 4, 5, 9, 51, 144-
     147
Kama-Mara, 29
Kant, E., 23
karma yoga, 59
Kelly, E., 37
Knudtson, P., 5, 49
Kohlberg, 10, 12
Koran, 137
Kornfield, Jack, viii, 26, 154, 157
Krippner, 43
Krishna, 57
Krishnamurti, 2, 58
kything, 70-71

Lao-tzu, 33, 35, 36
Larsen, Robin, 30, 40
law of compensation, 47
Lax, Bob, 111
LeShan, L., 54, 59
liberation, 7
lila, 153
Limits of Reason, The, 12
limits of growth, 12
linear and rational, 1
Locke, John, 98
locust position, 73
long-enduring mind, 56
love–animating principle of the
     universe, 39
lovingkindness meditation, 82-83,
     122
Lowell, James Russell, 97, 102
Luke, Helen, 38
lumen exterius, 22
lumen inferius, 22
lumen superius, 23
Lusseyran, Jacques, 48-49, 153
Lust, 30

ma, 148
macrocosm, 40

Macrorie, K., 25
management by objectives, 149
Man's Search for Meaning, 71
mantra, 3, 27, 58, 64-66, 122
mantram, 66
map of personal transformation, 29
Mara, 30
Marcel, Gabriel, 7
martial arts, 58
masculine/feminine, 9
material/sacred, 10
materialism, 13
matter and energy, 100
Matthiessen, Peter, 141
Matushita Corporation, 138
Maybury-Lewis, 46, 47
MBO (management by objectives),
   149
McAleer, John, 97, 101, 102
McKay, David, O., 137
meaning and interpretation, 11
mechanistic approaches, viii
meditatio, 23
meditation, viii, 26, 51-84
   and visualization to enhance
      performance, 145
   associated with medicine, 142
   in classrooms, 129
   on the breath, 122
   tool in relaxation process, 120
meditation, forms, 57-60
   action, 59-60
   emotional, 58
   intellectual, 58
   physical, 58-59
meditation/mindfulness, 148
meditative practice, 89
meditations, 60-83
   insight, 60-62
   lovingkindness, 82-84
   mantra, 65-66
   mindfulness, 62-65
   movement, 71-82
   visualization, 67-71
meditative stances, 54-57
   acceptance, 56
   being, not doing, 55

   big mind, long-enduring mind,
      56
   grace, 57
   openness, 54
   release, 55
Merton, Thomas, viii, 2, 24, 27, 87,
      109-115, 117, 157
metaphysics, 17
microcosm, 40
Miller, Jean, 157-162
mindfulness, 62-64, 148
Mitchell, Stephen, 35
model for business organizations,
      131
Moffett, James, 133
monomyth, 29
Moody, Raymond, 34, 152
Moses, 29
Mother Theresa, 59
Mott, Michael, 111, 114
movement meditation, 71-81
Mozart, 8, 113
multileveled realities, 34
Murphy, Michael, 4, 52, 139
Muslim, 65
mythology, 26

Nachmanovitch, Stephen, 155
nation/globe or region, 10
natural unfolding, 62
nature, 40
Navia, L. E., 37
Nehru, Motilal (Nehru's father),
      106
Nehru, Jawaharlal, 106
Neoplatonists, 98
New Age, 4
New Seeds of Contemplation, 112
new world order, 14
next level–mental, 24
Nicklaus, Jack, 139
Nine-Headed Dragon River, 139,
      141
nirvana, 87
non-visible world, 33
nondualistic experience, 3
Norton, Charles Eliot, 102
nutrition and exercise, 152

O'Connell, Greg, 145, 144
    meditation and experience with
    cancer, 146
Ontario Institute for Studies in
    Education (OISE), viii, 122,
    123, 154, 156
openness, 54
organic environment, 1
Ornish, Dean, 52, 152
outer/inner, 9
Over-Soul, 22, 41, 42, 99
Owen, 109

pace, or interval, *ma*, 150
paradise, 39
Pascale, R. T., 149, 150
path of transformation, 30
path with heart, 28
personal mastery, 9, 136, 137
perspective of Being, 23
Peters, Tom, 12, 135
peyote, 46
Phaedo, 37, 120
Philosopher of Democracy
    (Emerson), 94
physical meditation, 58-59
Piaget, 10, 12
Pibram, Karl, 45
Pining, 30
Plato, 33, 36-38, 40, 94, 96, 98,
    100, 119
    allegory of the cave, 3
    idea or form, 43
    invisible world, 33
Plotinus, 98
plow position, 79
Polanyi, M., 19
positivism, 17
positivistic assumptions, 17
Positivists, 18
presence, 21
psychotherapy and meditation,
    connection between, 147
purgatory, 38, 39

qualitative assessment, 11
quantity/quality, 9

Ram, 58
Ram Dass, viii, 150, 156
Rama, 108
rational approaches to education,
    law, and morality, 12
rational/intuitive, 9
realm of the invisible, 3
reason, intuits transcendent ideas,
    23
reflection-in-action, 19, 20, 23
Reflective Practitioner, The, 17
reflective conversation, 23
reflective practice, vii
release, 55
Republic, The, 36, 119
retribution, 47
Richards, Mary Caroline, 140, 141
    artistic mind, 141
Rifkin, J., 49
Right awareness, 90
    effort, 90
    livelihood, 90
    purpose, 90
    speech, 90
    understanding, 90
Rilke, T., 141
Ross, N. W., 90, 91
Rudolf Steiner Centre, 82

sacred moment, 2
sacred, 13
Sagan, Carl, 5
Salzburg, Sharon, 155
Samuels, M. & N., 69, 70
Saturn, 39
satyagraha, 104, 105
satyagrahri, 107
Savary, L. M., 70, 71
Schon, Donald, vii, 17, 18, 19, 20,
    24
Schubert, 8
Schulman, Arnold, 140
Schwartz, Gary, 51
scientific materialism, 6
Seat of the Soul, The, 157
second stage–system of aqueducts
    and waterwheel, 93

Seeds of Contemplation, The, 112
self, 2, 6, 24, 44, 138, 121
self-learning, 120
self-regulation, 51
self-union, 99
Senge, Peter, 9, 135, 136, 137
sensation, 99
sensibility, or sense experience, 23
Serpent King, 89
Seven Habits of Highly Effective People, The, 136
seven stages of contemplation, 93
Seven Storey Mountain, The, 112
shamanistic thinking, 45
Sharon, Douglas, 46
Sheehan, George, 139
shoulder stand, 77
Siddhartha Gautama (Buddha), 30, 87-91
Siegel, Bernie, 158
Siegel, Jessica, 25
Sign of Jonas, The, 113
Silananda, U., viii
silent prayer, 95
Singer, J., 34, 43, 44
sitting meditation, 122
skills and attitudinal component, 18
slowing down, 147
Smith, Huston, 59
Smuts, General Jan, 107
social action, 103
Socrates, 36
Soedjatmaoko, Dr., 114
solitude, 112
soul, 24
soul force, 104
source, 3
South Africa (Gandhi), 104-105
spacious awareness, 27
spirit, 45
spirit realm, 33
Spiritual Alphabet, The, 93
spiritual and philosophic quest for wisdom, 37
spiritual reality, 41
spontaneity or instinct, 99
spontaneous action, 106
St. Augustine, 92

St. Bonaventure, 22
Stearn, Jess (*Yoga, Youth and Reincarnation*), 156
Steindl-Rast, David, 3
stress reduction program, 142, 145
stress of teaching, 9
students daily journals, 123
subatomic physics, 44
Suinn, Richard, 140
Sujata, 88
supportive care program, 146
Suzuki, Roshi, 61
Suzuki, D. T., 5, 49, 113
Swedenborg, Emanuel, 34, 37, 40-41, 44, 4831
synthesis and contemplation, vii
systems, 45

tai chi, 58
Talbot, Michael, 40, 45
Tao, 3, 22, 33, 35-36, 39
Tao Te Ching, 35, 36
Taoism, 3
Tarnas, R., 10
Tart, C., 131
task oriented, 1
Teacher as Contemplative Practitioner, The, 122
technology/consciousness, 10
technical rationality, 17, 18
technological trance, 13
technology,
Teresa of Avila, viii, 87, 91-96, 115
themes from student journals, 127-131
Third Spiritual Alphabet, The, 92
third stage–river or spring, 94
Thoreau, Henry David, 98, 101, 155
thought and action, 91
three "eyes," 22-23
three levels nested, 23
Titmuss, Christopher, viii
Tolstoy, 20
transcendentalist, 41
Transcendentalists, 98
transforming experience, 8
Trappist monks, 111
Trowbridge, John, 97

Trungpa, 28
tribal wisdonm, 45
trusting heart, 52
Tukten, 141
twelve-point program, 53

Umland, Marcia, 25
understanding/conceptual and
    scientific intelligence, 23
universal myths, 28
University of Missouri at Kansas
    City (UMKC), 155
unmediated awareness, 25
untouchables, 105

Van Doren, Mark, 110, 111
Vaughan, 24
verifiability criterion, 19
Vienna Circle, 18
vipassana, insight meditation, 3, 60-
    62, 122
Virgil, 38, 39
visualization, 3, 67-71, 122

Walden, 98, 101
Way of Perfection, The, 94
way, the (Budhhism), 106
Wayne, John, 10
Weber, R., 45
Whelan, R., viii
Whitman, Walt, 98
Wilber, K., 22, 23, 24
Williams, Redford, 52
Winokur, J., 149, 152
Wirikuta, 46
witnessing, 151
Woodside, Don, 145, 146

Yeats, William, 160
yoga postures, 72-81
Yoga, Youth and Reincarnation,
    156
Young, Shinzen, 131, 148

zazen meditation, 61
Zen, 24, 25, 27, 145, 149, 159
Zukov, Gary (*The Seat of the Soul*),
    159

About the Author

JOHN P. MILLER is Head of the Field Centre of the Ontario Institute for Studies in Education in St. Catharines, Ontario. He is the author of *The Holistic Curriculum* (1988) and *The Compassionate Teacher* (1981).

ISBN 0-89789-401-4

90000>

EAN

9 780897 894012

HARDCOVER BAR CODE